D1611114

f e t i s h

The Princeton Architectural Journal

Volume 4

EDITORS:
Sarah Whiting
Edward Mitchell
Greg Lynn
MANAGING EDITOR:
Patrick Deaton
TEXT EDITOR:
Lois Nesbitt
DESIGN:
Greg Lynn—Edward Mitchell
except *Mouseion* by the author

The Princeton Journal is published and distributed by Princeton Architectural Press, 37 East 7th Street, New York, New York 10003. For back issues of The Princeton Journal write to Princeton Architectural Press, Send editorial correspondence to The Princeton Journal, School of Architecture, Princeton University, Princeton, New Jersey 08544.

ISBN 0-910413-92-4
ISSN 074-1-1774
Cover illustration: Clara Peeters. Private collection, USA.

$\mathcal{T}$ ABLE OF CONTENTS

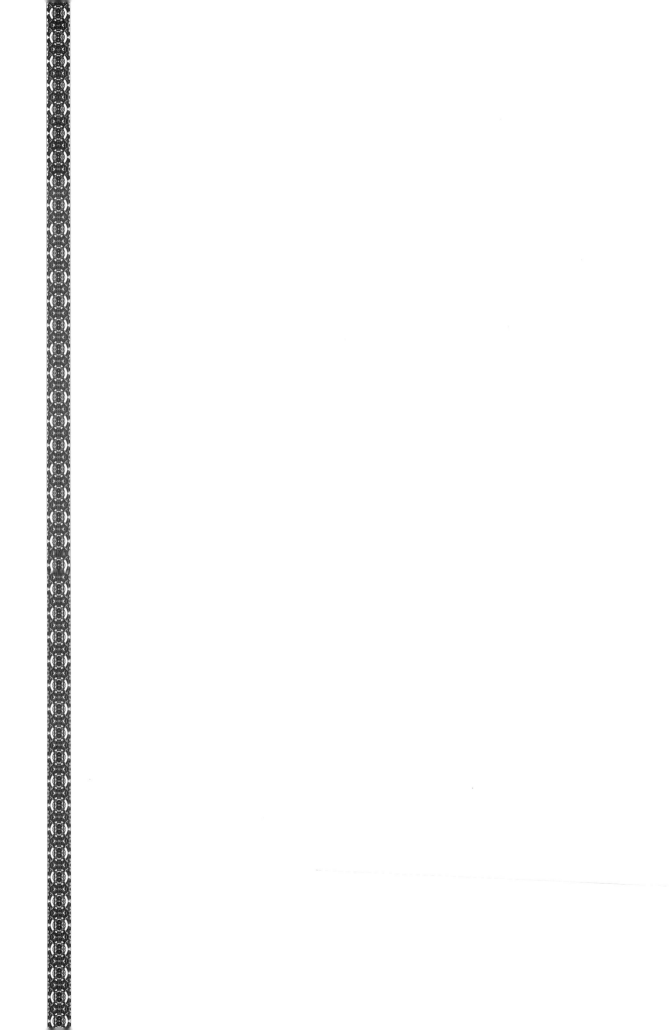

$\mathcal{M}$ARX, ADORNO, BENJAMIN, AND BAUDRILLARD have all used the term "fetish" in reference to the commodity culture resulting from a capitalist economy and society. In his essay, "The Fetish Character in Music and Regression of Listening," Adorno describes the devaluation of music through the replacement of qualitative musical value with consumptive, commercial value: "what makes its appearance," he writes, "is the exchange-value in which the quantum of possible enjoyment has disappeared." Freud uses the term as a repressive counterfeit when he defines the fetish as "a substitute which blocks or displaces a traumatic discovery of loss." In choosing the topic of the fetish for Volume IV of *The Princeton Journal*, we hoped to examine these aspects of the fetish—commodity and counterfeit—as they apply to architecture and urbanism.

At one point during the Fetishism Conference the subject of the day's events were paraphrased by Jeffrey Kipnis with the question: "Can we really take up the question of the fetish without repeating the problem?" Indeed, binding the topic of the fetish within this issue of *The Princeton Journal: Thematic Studies in Architecture*, inevitably runs the risk of fetishizing theory not only through the creation of a precious object that replaces the discussion it covers, but further by yet again importing a concept—this time the concept of the fetish itself—into architectural discourse.

Yet, this book is suspiciously ornamental and excessively displays itself as an object. In this sense it is intended to participate in the introduction of the discussion of the fetish to architecture. However, as the ornamental structure of the book interferes with the content which it houses, so did the outnumbered architects interfere with the introduction of the fetish to their discipline, arguing that it was itself already present within the process of design. It is unfortunate that the extension of this discussion—of architecture's preclusion to look outside itself for its own description, which was primarily argued by the architects Kipnis and Robert Somol—occurred after the event of the conference with the additions of papers by Ann Bergren, Jennifer Bloomer and Mark Wigley. It is hoped that the publication of this volume will extend this discussion further.

Several people should be thanked for their help in putting together both the conference and the publication. All of the symposium participants went far beyond their duties as speakers in helping us guide this discussion. Emily Apter deserves particular credit. The faculty at Princeton University should be thanked for their role as discussants in the symposium: Beatriz Colomina, Alan Colquhoun, Robert Maxwell, Anthony Vidler, and Mark Wigley. Thank you to the patience of Dean Ralph Lerner and the support of past Dean Robert Maxwell, without which the conference and journal would not have been possible. John Nichols Studio should also be thanked for the printing of the symposium poster. Thanks to Wallis Miller and Patricia Morton for their help during the symposium, to Kevin Lippert and Ann Urban of Princeton Architectural Press, and to Lisa Govan and Joe Freedman of Sarabande Press. Finally, we would like to thank the Mellon Foundation and the School of Architecture at Princeton University for their generous financial support of the symposium and the publication.

HAL FOSTER

The Art of Fetishism: Notes on Dutch Still Life

Oysters, lemon pulp, heavy goblets full of dark wine, long clay pipes, gleaming chestnuts, pottery, tarnished metal cups, three grape seeds—what can be the justification of such an assemblage if not to lubricate man's gaze amid his domain, to facilitate his daily business among objects whose riddle is dissolved and which are no longer anything but easy surfaces? —Roland Barthes

 O ROLAND BARTHES WRITES of seventeenth-century Dutch still life, and I believe he is correct: this is a primary goal of such still life. But it is rarely achieved, for the gaze of the viewer and the riddle of objects are not so easily treated. In this art the gaze is less lubricated than fixed (as in the Freudian scenario of sexual fetishism), and the riddle of objects is less solved than posed again and again (as in the Marxian metaphor of commercial fetishism whereby commodities appear as "hieroglyphs" in "the riddle" of our own social labor). To argue this is to advance both a general thesis and a methodological approach: that, far from a golden mean, Dutch still life expresses an anxiety about the gaze and a confusion about the value of objects and that the best way to explore this structure of feeling is through the discourse of fetishism.

At first glance it may seem anachronistic to relate the discourse of fetishism to Dutch still life, yet seventeenth-century Holland is a crucial site of its articulation. On a general level, the composite figure of the fetishist drawn by Marx and Freud—the capitalist patriarch—is first fully developed at this time and place, and on a local level Dutch still life manifests too many of the attributes commonly associated with fetishism not to be considered, at least in part, in its terms. The three primary models of fetishism—anthropological, Marxian and Freudian—all define the fetish as an object endowed with a special force or independent life (Marx writes explicitly of "transference," Freud of "overvaluation"). Too many viewers have remarked upon the strange energy that emanates from the objects of Dutch still life (my references will be mostly to *pronk* modes) for us not to admit a connection. If only a superficial sheen or shine, this intensity cannot be explained away as an effect of a disguised symbolism or as a residue of a religious gaze; a fetishistic projection on the part of artist and viewer alike is involved. Often in Dutch still life the inert appears animate, the insignificant seems humanly, even preternaturally, significant (the Greek term for still life is translated "rhyparography," the depiction of insignificant things), and the familiar becomes estranged.

1.

Now in one way or another these effects are attributes of fetishism not only in the anthropological sense but also in the Marxian and Freudian senses. Marx argued that in commodity exchange people and things trade semblances: social relations take on the character of object relations and commodities assume the active agency of people. An inkling of this inversion of subject-object relations is evident in many Dutch still lifes—as if the objects were endowed with life to the degree that the viewer is sapped of it. Similarly, Freud argued that in experiences of the uncanny, which he related specifically to castration anxiety and its fetishistic defense, animate and inanimate states are confused, things are subsumed by representations, once homey images return as *unheimlich,* and a whiff or whisper of death hangs over the scene. Again, many of these qualities are present in Dutch still life. Indeed, the insistence of such terms as still life, *still leven,* and *nature morte,* all of which refer to the stilled state of the motif, suggests an anxiety that it might be otherwise—that there is an uncanny animation, a fetishistic projection, active here. It hardly suffices to read such attributes in(to) such painting, but that is not really my purpose. Rather, I want to propose that the very dynamics of fetishism, at least as described in its three primary models, structure this art. I will begin with the anthropological account and then proceed to the Marxian and Freudian conceptions.

The term "fetish" derives from the Portuguese *feitico;* it was used first in relation to witchcraft and then, adopted by fifteenth-century Portuguese traders, in relation to the cult objects of West Africans. This is the origin of the common anthropological meaning of the

2.

fetish as a thing possessed of a (super)natural quality or force. Less well known is its elaboration by seventeenth-century Dutch merchants who had ousted the Portuguese from the Gold and Slave coasts by 1642, or roughly the high point of the Dutch still-life tradition. In this case African fetishes were related directly to Catholic sacramental objects; in 1602 Marees compares "Fetissos" to saints (it was he who introduced the term to northern Europe), and in 1704 Willem Bosman wrote:

> If it was possible to convert the Negroes to the Christian Religion, the Roman-Catholicks
> would succeed better than we should, because they already agree in several particulars,
> especially in their ridiculous ceremonies.

This, of course, is a Protestant claim: to deny that any material object has a special capacity of spiritual mediation. But in this religious point is hidden an economic agenda: to denounce as primitive and infantile the refusal to assess value rationally, to trade objects in a system of equivalence—in short, to submit to capitalist exchange. (Note that in this proto-Enlightenment discourse the great hybrid figure of modern ideology—the savage-child-madman—is already announced.) As an irrational relation to objects, fetishism was not just an abomination in the eyes of the Lord; it was also a damned nuisance to market activity. To an extent, then, Dutch object relations in the seventeenth century were articulated in relation to fetishism, Catholic and African, in such a way as to privilege not only Protestant individualism but also commodity exchange. And still-life can be seen as one important site where this new, contradictory complex of subject-object relations was mediated and expressed.

There is an irony here, however, that can also be read in the art: as religious fetishism was suppressed, a commercial fetishism, a fetishism of the commodity, was released; the Dutch denounced one overvaluation of objects only to produce another of their own. For Marx commodity fetishism is analogous to religious projection. I want to argue one step further: that commodity fetishism partly replaced religious fetishism or at least compensated for its partial loss. This displacement-overvaluation is symbolically enacted in pronk still lifes: even today, positioned reverently before these gold chalices, fine porcelain pieces, and exquisite glasses like so many worshippers before the golden calf, we might believe, as perhaps did the Dutch, that these things have a mana of their own—a mana, moreover, that redounds to the mana or value of painting. For baroque artists, in particular still-life practitioners, the nobility of painting, its art value, was hardly secure. Thus it was important to display that the art of painting could go beyond other crafts, that the value of the work could subsume other values. In this agenda painting was to become the ultimate golden calf—as it is for us today, as it had begun to be for the seventeenth-century Dutch.

My point is not simply that the Dutch, in default of fetishistic religious icons, fetishized objects of exchange, especially (in) paintings. It is more importantly that they employed fetishism as a category with which to negotiate the different economies of the object that they encountered in the course of market expansion. Pronk still lifes in particular seem like tabulations or mappings of the most diverse objects from the most disparate classes and cultures. A given painting by De Heem or Kalf may include not only metalware from Nurnberg and glass from Venice but also porcelain from China, tobacco from America, shells from the Far East, rugs from the Near East, exotic spices from the Indian archipelago, and so on: so many synecdoches, if not of the Dutch empire, then at least of the Dutch market. Often these synecdoches threaten to burst open the circumscribed space of traditional still life, the limited scene of its domestic setting, to outside other worlds. But that is a necessary risk, for *fig. 1* it appears that the objects of disparate classes and cultures are depicted precisely so that they *fig. 2* may be mastered in representation, so that the domestic space and capitalist subjectivity of the seventeenth-century Dutch may be secured from its outside and its others by a synecdochic incorporation of these very things. It is this fetishism—fetishism as a negotiation of divergent representations and dangerous realities—that pronk still life embodies.

Such negotiations must also be made within cultures, and Dutch still life operates in this arena too. For instance, there is a tension, especially as the focus of the tradition passes from meal themes to pronk motifs, among objects of direct use, objects produced for exchange, and objects of display or prestation. In early still lifes use objects predominate, and they are generally depicted matter-of-factly (as Marx says, there is nothing mysterious about them). In later still lifes objects of exchange and/or display predominate, and they are often *fig. 5* represented in a mystificatory way (at once phantasmagorical and palpable, as Marx notes of *fig. 3* commodities). The difference in these types cannot be ascribed only to different artistic *fig. 6* subjects, styles, milieux; it also concerns different social aspects of the economy differently

apprehended. This apparent transition from paintings primarily of use objects to paintings primarily of exchange and/or display objects may well reflect the increased presence of the market as a mediator of Dutch social life in the seventeenth century—and the increased pressure on pictorial representation to come to terms with it, to articulate its different objects, registers, levels. Of course, commodity production was hardly total as yet, but it was general enough to effect regimes of vision and modes of representation, and we can see the effects in certain still lifes: often it is as if natural things like flowers and shells, or useful objects like knives and glasses, are coated with the shellac of commodity status before our very eyes—as if the painter were compelled to endow them with a pictorial value to match the commercial value that they had already acquired on the market (a double "speculation" seems operative here). Fetishism is thus almost a mandate: in order to reassure patrons, to secure value, objects

fig. 7
fig. 3
must be represented as if value were inherent in them (the intensive pictorial elaboration of flowers and shells suggests this). In pronk still lifes in particular natural and useful objects do
fig. 8
not bear the physical marks of the hand so much as they trace the value machinations of the market. The transformation, however, is never complete: old referents, contexts, subject-object relations remain. As a result, the objects often seem caught in between worlds, not
fig. 9
dead, not alive, not useful, not useless. And the pictorial effect is often one of deathly
fig. 4
suspension or, as remarked before, of eerie animation, as if the objects were at once chilled
fig. 10
and charged by the speculative gaze of the painter and the patron.

This pall is occasionally cast over meal pieces, too, and the effect is to invert the structure of feeling implicit in the genre since its beginnings. Extant Greek still lifes mostly depict food, as do many Roman examples; still life was designated a *xenion*, a present made

3.

to a guest. In its purported origins, then, still life was less about display than it was about offering: it represented a gift exchange. Such gift exchange is only residual in a commodity system, and the structure of feeling, the welcome if you like, of the still-life genre is adversely affected. Certainly in pronk pieces the concern with social position—with excess and ostentation—or, even less generous, the emphasis on moral probity—on "remonstrance against excess and ostentation"—overwhelms the sense of offering or gift vestigial in still life. The offering is somehow denied before the fact; the gift has a social, moral, or economic tag attached; the presentation intimidates more than welcomes. Again the chill of the commodity is felt—and in heretofore removed spaces. For just as the new market invades the intimate space of the still life, so too it erodes the old Aristotelian distinction between the economy of the household and the accumulation of value through commerce; and directly or indirectly many still lifes comment on this penetration.

fig. 14

fig. 15

     The becoming-commodity of things produces other paradoxes as well. On the one hand, as the market becomes more *in*tensive, objects are referred to the order of money; they become, in principle or potential at least, more equivalent. On the other hand, as the market becomes more *ex*tensive, objects become more diverse. Is it too much to suggest that pronk still life negotiates this apparent paradox too? Whether in the more monochromatic style of the 1620s and 1630s (usually referred to moral imperatives alone) or in the more coloristic modes thereafter, the representational grid of the typical still life becomes not only more pictorially consistent but also more referentially porous to objects of all sorts. Indeed, such paintings often appear as sites that can accommodate almost any kind of represented thing (natural or culinary, homemade or elaborate, mundane or exotic). Is there a logic to this

4.

5.

tabulation of difference within sameness, or is the effect not one of heterotopia? Certainly there seems little taxonomic logic either to the typical pronk still life or to its more artisanal cousin, the cabinet of curiosities (whether actual or depicted). The principle of order here cannot be found in the nature of the objects alone, and the transcendental guarantee of God no longer appears automatically. Rather, the primary plane of consistency is the shared status of the things as more or less precious or rare commodities. (Paintings fit this category of commodity-collectible too, and they are often included in curio cabinets and represented in still lifes.) It is this common condition that allows for the difference within sameness in the still lifes: diverse objects can be brought together in these paintings because they are *already* brought together not so much in the domestic space as on the marketplace—they already exist to be exchanged, collected, consumed. The ultimate principle of order in Dutch still life, then, may well be the imperial market: it is a first support and a final referent of this art. (This suggestion may in turn lend credence to the otherwise outlandish claim that the fall of the metaphoric or symbolic tabulation of objects in religious art coincides with the rise of a metonymic or synecdochic tabulation in capitalist art.)

Of course, art does not simply submit to economic logic; along with myriad other things, it can expose or mediate contradictions within an economy. Painting for the open market was common in mid-seventeenth-century Holland, and there was a high division of artistic labor. Whether or not one subscribes to the old saw that scarcity of land encouraged speculation in pictures, it does appear that the Dutch were generally at ease with the status of art as commodity and investment. Certainly the value of paintings was subject to the

6.

7.

8.

9.

fluctuations of the market and the whims of speculation. Yet there was a tension or negotiation here as well. I noted the negotiation within pronk sill lifes between objects of use and exchange value; a related negotiation occurs around the paintings between value fixed according to labor time (in the old guild manner) and value determined by the marketplace. This negotiation of values was very important for the mid-seventeenth-century Dutch (witness the tulip mania),

10.

11.

12.

13.

and once again pronk still life was a symbolically significant site of such negotiation: indirectly, in its making, still life allowed the Dutch to think the pros and cons of different kinds of value creation. So too in its styles and subjects, still life enabled the Dutch to reflect on the related ethical-economic tension between control and consumption. As Simon Schama argues in *The Embarrassment of Riches*, this issue was hardly black-and-white morally or economically:

better expenditure, it was felt, than avarice; better circulation than accumulation. Like the contemporary Reaganomic consumer, the seventeenth-century Dutch subject was positioned schizophrenically: moral restraint and economic expenditure were both encouraged. Pronk still life was asked to represent these imperatives simultaneously: thus its negotiation between order and disorder, godliness and greed—a negotiation that helps to explain otherwise conceptually conflicted tableaux such as a spilled chalice immaculately composed or a spoiled *fig. 11* pie exquisitely glazed. The viewer may revel in this consumption but sees it configured and controlled—not only by composition and chastisement (the destructive excess, the implicit vanitas) but also by skilled craft. The productive labor of the artist and the measured value of the work helped to assuage anxiety about affluence, expenditure, speculation—and so, in some sense, abetted these activities. In any case, in pictorial art as in economic society there existed an interplay between spending and saving, luxury and frugality, an attraction toward the sovereignty of possession and a renunciation of this possessive sovereignty, and still life was called upon to work through this general contradiction between "acquisitiveness and asceticism"—in effect, to caution the subject about the two extremes but allow him to have it both ways. Still life treated these extremes not only in its subjects, compositions, and craft but in its stylistic development, which oscillated between "acquisitive" and "ascetic" poles.

Such a great cultural contradiction cannot, of course, be resolved in art, but it can be expressed or intuited there. By way of conclusion I want to suggest that Dutch still life treats such anxieties but cannot finally assuage them. In part it fails to do so because it produces an anxiety of its own, and in order to understand this effect it is useful to turn to the third primary model of fetishism, that of Freud. For Freud the fetish is a substitute for the (maternal) penis thought to be castrated; it screens out this "castration" and so blocks its threat. But fetishism is not only disavowal: it is a compromise-formation that allows the subject to have it both ways: to see the woman (the mother) as both whole and castrated. As such, the fetish is also a "memorial" (as Freud says) to castration. Now my point is not to relate the ambivalence of seventeenth-century Dutch society regarding material culture directly to this ambivalence of the fetishist. Rather, I want to suggest that Dutch still life is, like the Freudian fetish, a structure of ambivalence that tends to a splitting of the ego of the viewer (as Freud argues regarding the most neurotic fetishists) even though it is disposed to his mastery. In many ways Dutch still life is perfect—perfectly composed, perfectly finished—with no hint of lack or loss. We may look at these shiny canvases as an infant of six-to-eighteen months is said to look at a mirror—with relief that the image reflected there is made whole. But this perfection may hide a preexistent loss or "castration." (Could this be a reason why finish is such a fetish in this and other art?) Moreover, this perfection may reflect our gaze in a way that finally threatens it. Possessed of this art, of its material riches and visual splendors, we may also be threatened with dispossession. (At a more obvious level, meal and pronk still lifes are often so abundant as to deny the very possibility of incompletion—and yet right before our eyes, in the guise of a split *fig. 12* peach or a cut wedge of cheese, there may lie a displaced image of "castration"). *fig. 13*

The mini case history that Freud presents in his 1927 "Fetishism" essay may help to clarify the stakes here. He tells us of a young man who, born in an English environment but raised in a German one, fetishized a "shine on the nose." Now this *Glanz auf der Nase*, Freud writes, "was in reality a 'glance at the nose.' The nose was thus the fetish, which, incidentally, he endowed at will with the luminous shine which was not perceptible to others." There is

14.

much to develop here, but Freud does little with it: intent on the formula of the fetish as (maternal) phallic substitute, he does not listen to his own analysand. So what actually happens in this case? The man fetishizes a shine on a nose of a woman; that is, with his gaze a male subject projects onto a female object the condition of loss or "castration." This suggests that the loss preexists her in him; she is simply his projected representation of it. In short, the "castration" is his; and, indeed, many losses or separations (maternal breast, feces, etc.) precede the hypothetical sighting of castration—even if they are understood as such only retrospectively through this optic. It is this preexistent loss in the subject that demands fetishistic perfection in the object, and this dynamic, I believe, is operative in much "art appreciation." More importantly, though the fetishistic displacement of glance to *Glanz* is linguistic, the fetishistic projection is visual: the glance is projected by the subject onto the object, which returns this gaze as a *Glanz*, a "luminous shine which was not perceptible to others." I suggested above that the capitalistic gaze of the Dutch subject endows the object with a special luminous life; here the fetishistic gaze of the Dutch subject can be seen to project a similar "shine." (Could it be that artistic aura in general is produced by this very projection/reflection of the regard of the painter/viewer?)

The question then becomes: why might this glance-*Glanz* be received by the subject as a threat? There are at least two reasons, one of which is suggested in the notion that the fetish is also a memorial to castration. As a fetishistic projection, the glance-*Glanz* might include a reminder of the very loss that haunts the subject. Certainly still life seems so marked: a ghost of a lack hangs over its very abundance. The second reason concerns the psychical association of the threat of castration with the threat of blindness (which, again, is made explicit by Freud in his essay on the uncanny). More than any other genre, perhaps, still life is disposed for our gaze. And yet the very intensity of our gaze causes it to be reflected: pronk pictures in particular seem to return our look, so to speak. Others have remarked upon a similar effect in perspective: as equal and opposite to the viewpoint, the vanishing point seems to double our gaze, to return it; it threatens our gaze with its alienated double, threatens us with the nullity that it, the vanishing point, represents. I want to suggest that this effect is also often produced in still life, even though one might argue that still life is precisely the form pledged against perspective. In Dutch still life it is as if we are seen as we see; only in this case, it is objects that "see" us. Disposed for our gaze, still life, no less than perspectival construction, threatens to dispossess us of our sight. Our gaze, made intense, even Medusal, in still life looks back from things and threatens us. (Could it be that the intensity of the gaze, perhaps religious in origin, has nowhere to go but to return to the subject once freed of its transcendental anchor in God?) This anxiety, this ambivalence, is fundamental to Dutch still life; it is the ambivalence to which the other ambivalences produced by the genre and its objects—as tokens of different classes and exotic lands, as examples of the strange new form of the commodity—must finally be referred.

15.

Footnotes

1. Roland Barthes, "The World as Object," *Calligram: Essays in New Art History from France*, ed. Norman Bryson (Cambridge: Cambridge University Press, 1988), 108.
2. For a reading of anthropological fetishism, see William Pietz, "The Problem of the Fetish, I & II," *Res 9* and *13* (Spring 1985 and Spring 1987), 5–17 and 23–45. My understanding of fetishism is greatly enhanced by his genealogy of the term. Also see my "(Dis)Agreeable Objects" in *Damaged Goods* (New York: New Museum of Contemporary Art, 1985).
3. Panofsky suggested a mutuality of naturalist observation and religious symbolism in early Netherlandish painting. Ingvar Bergstrom elaborates this insight into a general interpretation of Dutch still life, "Certain artists were attempting to separate the customary symbols from the religious scene and to give them an independent existence as a symbolical still life," *Dutch Still Life Painting* (London, 1956), 14. To my mind this is necessary but not sufficient.
4. Willem Bosman, *A New and Accurate Description of the Coast of Guinea* (London: Cass, 1967), 154. Both Marees and Bosman are quoted in Pietz, "The Problem of the Fetish, II," 39. Interestingly, "fetishism" referred to an other within—female peasant "witches"—before it was projected to an other without—the West African tribespeople. The later association of the concept with an adversary within—the "Roman-Catholics"—suggests again that fetishism concerns the encounter between systems of objects rather than the specific nature of any one system.
5. See Pietz, "The Problem of the Fetish II," 41.
6. See Charles Sterling, *Still Life Painting: From Antiquity to the Twentieth Century* (New York: Harper and Row), 28.
7. Sven Segal, *A Prosperous Past: The Sumptuous Still Life in the Netherlands 1600–1700* (The Hague: SDU Publishers, 1988), 169.
8. See Svetlana Alpers, *Rembrandt's Enterprise: The Studio and the Market* (Chicago: University of Chicago Press, 1988), 96.
9. Simon Schama reads Dutch still life too directly in these terms: the Monochrome breakfast pieces are said to express humanist balance, the colorful pronk ostentatious display. But it is pointless to deny the emphasis. In fact, it suggests another economic value represented in still life—sumptuous value, or still life as the site of prestige garnered through expenditure. After all, one of the meanings of *pronken* is "to show off" (Segal translates its pictorial derivative as "sumptuous still life"), and Schama notes that Dutch culture had "a rich tradition of ceremonial waste" *(The*

Embarrassment of Riches: An Interpretation of Dutch Culture in the Golden Age [Berkeley: University of California Press, 1988], 310).

10. Schama, *The Embarrassment of Riches*, 338. Schama suggests that Dutch culture dealt with this ambivalence: "This moral pulling and pushing may have made for inconsistency, but it did not much confuse the artisan, the merchant or the banker in their daily affairs. The peculiar coexistence of apparently opposite value systems was what they expected of their culture," 371. But ambivalence is not so readily treated.

11. As noted, "fetishism" commonly refers to a supernatural quality in an object. However, the term derives from the Latin *factitius*, which means manufactured, artificial, factitious, or fraudulent. There is thus a doubleness of the natural and the artificial concealed in the term. A related doubleness is active in Dutch still life, particularly in its finish, which was intended to signal both natural perfection and skilled artifice (see Alpers, *Rembrandt's Enterprise*, 98). This doubleness may be related to the fetishistic structure of classical representation in general, which both affirms and disavows the objectness of the painting and the presence of the viewer.

12. Sigmund Freud, "Fetishism," *On Sexuality* (London: Penguin Books, 1977), 351.

13. Barthes extends this principle to cover all seventeenth-century Dutch art. Is it coincidental that the great glazes of the still lifes are contemporaries of the great gazes of the group portraits? Barthes writes: "It is the gaze that is the *numen* here, the gaze that disturbs, intimidates, and makes man the ultimate term of the problem," "The World as Object, " 119.

14. See Norman Bryson, *Tradition & Desire: From David to Delacroix* (Cambridge: Cambridge University Press, 1984), 63–84. My reading of Dutch still life is enhanced by conversations with Bryson, whose book on still life, *Looking at the Overlooked*, is forthcoming.

Contemporary investigations of the gaze focus on matters of perspective. In the neo-Kantian tradition of art history, Renaissance perspective is seen as the reconciliation of subject and object (Panofsky), as a form devoted to the mastery of the viewer. Contemporary readings see it instead as a potential crisis for the subject. To my mind, much baroque painting can be seen as an implicit response to the castrative charge of Renaissance perspective—as so many attempts to render it opaque or to diffuse it through excessive elaboration. Dutch still life can also be seen as such a defense , yet it is precisely here that the repressed returns. Still life overcomes the threat implicit in the gaze of the perspective, only to reproduce it in another form—in the look of the object. As Jean Baudrillard writes of trompe-l'oeil objects: " in trompe l'oeil the effect of perspective is somehow thrown forward . . . Nothing to see: it is things that see you, they do not fly from you, they bear themselves before you like your own hallucinated interiority," "The Trompe–L'Oeil," *Calligram*, 58. Perhaps this is intuited in certain Dutch still lifes; certainly there are moves that might be construed as defenses against it. For example, the more monochromatic compositions of the 1620s and 1630s, especially those of Peter Claesz and William Claesz, not only suggest moral moderation or economic equivalence but mute the gaze, relieve it of its Medusal intensity, free the subject from his own scopic fascination/fixation/fetishism. So too does the more painterly style of van Beyeren and the colorful saturation of the glutted object field of De Heem—this last can disorder or scatter the gaze, blocking its reflected return.

Illustrations

EMILY APTER

Specularity and Reproduction: Marx, Freud, Baudrillard

Culture is refuse, whereas art is truth, but only phenomenally, that is, as appearance. The reason behind this is to be found in the dual essence of fetishism.—*Theodor Adorno*, Aesthetic Theory

*I*N HIS CHAPTER ON FETISHISM and ideology in *For a Critique of the Political Economy of the Sign*, Jean Baudrillard characterized the term fetishism as almost having "a life of its own." "Instead of functioning as a metalanguage for the magical thinking of others," he argued, "it turns against those who use it, and surreptitiously exposes their own magical thinking."[1] Baudrillard here identifies the uncanny retroactivity of fetishism as a theory, its strange ability to hex the user through the haunting inevitability of a "deconstructive turn."

Neither Marx nor Freud managed to escape the return of the repressed fetish. Freud endowed the fetish of the (castrated) maternal phallus with an animus when he wrote: "It seems rather, that when the fetish comes to life, so to speak, some process has been suddenly interrupted—it reminds one of the abrupt halt made by memory in traumatic amnesias."[2] Marx, endeavoring in *Capital* to define the "commodity fetish," lures the reader into a labyrinth of discomfiting allusions. "A commodity appears, at first sight, a very trivial thing, and easily understood" he begins, only to retract: "Its analysis shows that it is, in reality, a very queer thing, abounding in metaphysical subtleties and theological niceties."[3] The same paragraph ends on an even more fantastic note, when an ordinary table, transformed into a "commodity," "evolves out of its wooden brain grotesque ideas, far more wonderful than 'table-turning.' "[4] If here the metaphor is table-turning, later the mysterious value of the fetish commodity floats before the eye like an apparition. After constructing an optical analogy for the relation between man and commodity, Marx advises "recourse to the mist-enveloped regions of the religious world."[5] Alternately confusing and conflating appearance and reality; *Eidos* and materialism; alienation and belief, Marx, according to W. J. T. Mitchell, "disabled" his discourse through the very mastertropes that gave his arguments the power to imprint themselves on the political unconscious.[6] If the *camera obscura* was his preferred figure for ideology and fetishism his preferred figure for commodities, then the two terms were frequently "crossed," for, as Mitchell points out, both

1. *2.*

3.

signify false images: the former connoting an "idol of the mind" and the latter, in Francis Bacon's wording, an "idol of the marketplace." At some level, these idols become indistinguishable, rendering commodities dangerously interchangeable with the "true" currency of ideas. Mirroring each other as "icons" of illusion, both tropes, according to Mitchell, ultimately subvert their author's attempt at demystification. "Ideology and fetishism," he ascertains, "have taken a sort of revenge on Marxist criticism, insofar as it has made a fetish out of the concept of fetishism, and treated ideology as an occasion for the elaboration of a new idealism."[7]

Now even if we disagree with Mitchell's conclusion that Marxist criticism has reified the elements of its own theory or allowed fetishism to masquerade as demystification, it does seem true that within contemporary discourse there is a kind of fetishism in the air. And this metaleptic or hypertropic character is hardly confined to Marxist usage—it seems, as Baudrillard suggests, endemic to fetishism's history as a metaphysical construct. In my remarks here I want to examine briefly the history of fetishism as a theory emphasizing: (1) its simultaneous critique of and implication in the very sociosymbolic phenomena that it

seeks to unveil (from commodification to castration anxiety); (2) its importance as a specular meeting point for psychoanalytic and materialist discourses; and (3) its implications for a radical theoretical praxis in the domain of contemporary aesthetic production.

fig. 4

In the course of its etymological life from its Chaucerian prehistory to its post-Enlightenment usage in the twentieth century, the word *fetisso* and its phonological cognates has provoked a chain of divergent interpretations, all generated according to the codes of a Romance linguistics forced to accept the untranslatable Other into its thoroughly Western genealogy. Used in the eighteenth century by the Président de Brosses (dubbed by Voltaire "the little fetish" for his pains) to describe the idolatrous worship of material objects in "primitive" societies, the term was traced to *fatum*, signifying both fate and charm. A century later the British ethnologist Edward Tylor derived the term from a different though related root (*factitius*) comprising both the "magic arts" and the "work of art."[8] The Italian philosopher Giorgio Agamben, following Marx (fetishism of commodities as false consciousness) and Freud (the fetish as spurious, surrogate object of desire) deduced from the Latin *facere* neither charm nor beauty but rather the degraded simulacrum or false representation of things sacred, beautiful, or enchanting.[9]

Though a semantic disjunction clearly emerges each time the word fetishism is displaced from language to language, discipline to discipline, and culture to culture, it is

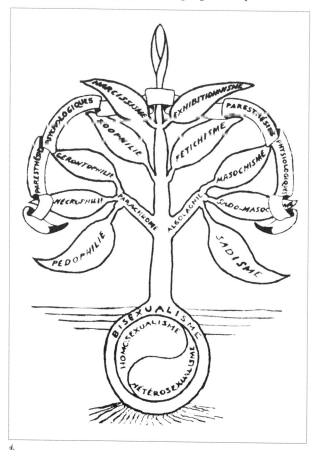

4.

precisely this process of creative mistranslation that endows the term with its value as currency of literary exchange, as verbal token. Thus the word *charme*, used by Stéphane Mallarmé and Paul Valéry to denote the incantatory power of music (*carmen*: "psalm," "oracle," "sacred song"), was seen as the carrier of an authentic neoprimitivism; a sign linking symbolism to an exotic repertory of votive objects including the "gri-gri," the "juju," and the "phiphob" (cf. Tylor). Like a good-luck charm or native artifact offered to the European traveler, the verbal fetish, surrounded by the aura of otherness, was aestheticized by the French poets of the turn of the century from Mallarmé to Victor Segalen, Blaise Cendrars and Guillaume Apollinaire. As *fetys* ("well-made, beautiful") the fetish emerged as a catalyst of symbolist artifice; as *fatum* or fateful chance (*le hasard*) it recalled the master-narratives of shipwreck, solitude, and confrontation between the civilized and "savage" mind from *Robinson Crusoe* to *"Un coup de dés";* and as "Christs of another form, another belief, inferior Christs of obscure wishes" in Apollinaire's poem "Zone" (1912) it became a proto-surrealist icon, mediating between urban *anomie* and a "fantom Africa" (cf. Michel Leiris).[10]

If the literary history of fetishism reveals a discursive pattern of difference, its philosophical history deconstructs in the form of a rhetorical chiasmus. William Pietz has given us the most historically nuanced account of the philosophical fetish, which, he argues, points to the "emerging articulation of a theoretical materialism quite incompatible and in conflict with the philosophical tradition."[11] Following his scheme, it appears that from Kant (fetishism as a degraded sublime, a "trifle") and Hegel (fetishism as a "factitious universal," an unmediated particular) to Whitehead ("a fallacy of misplaced concreteness") and Heidegger ("an Ereigenes, an appropriation") fetishism has been portrayed as theoretically worthless.[12] As a word it was not even admitted into the French language by the Académie Francaise until 1835. But it is just this quantity of negative value that ultimately enables fetishism to undermine monolithic belief structures from Christianity and Enlightenment philosophy to the "rational" laws of capitalist exchange. For example, the Portuguese trading word *fetisso* stood not just for the native idol but also for the small wares or trinkets that European merchants used for barter or upon which they swore oaths to honor commercial transactions. According to Pietz, these trading rituals inevitably led to:

> . . . *a perversion of the natural processes of economic negotiation and legal contact. Desiring a clean economic interaction, seventeenth-century merchants unhappily found themselves entering into social relations and quasi-religious ceremonies that should have been irrelevant to the conduct of trade.*[13]

Pietz's argument implies that Africa perverted Western capitalism (forcing it to adopt the superstitious worship of material objects) just as European capitalists perverted indigenous economies through exploitation. One may further deduce from this historico-philosophical chiasmus two central consequences: first, that the "civilized" mimesis of "primitive" object worship was only the explicit acting out of Europe's own (masked)

5.

fig. 5

commodity fetishism; and second that, almost as a result of Europe's initial contempt for tribal artifacts, the exotic fetish returned to continental shores where it was henceforth recommodified as art.

Each of these problematics inflected the conditions of what James Clifford has characterized as "ethnographic surrealism":

> *For the Paris avant-garde, Africa, (and to a lesser degree, Oceania and America) provided a reservoir of other forms and other beliefs. This suggests a second element of the ethnographic surrealist attitude, a belief that the Other (whether accessible in dreams, fetishes, or Lévy-Bruhl's mentalité primitive) was a crucial object of modern research.*[14]

Clifford enumerates the ways in which Africa was decoded and recoded in Europe, a process effected, to a great extent, through an "artsy" appropriation of the display techniques employed in the ethnographic museum. Walter Benjamin, citing Taine ("L'Europe s'est déplacé pour voir des marchandises" ["The whole of Europe displaced itself in order to view the goods"]), has provided the most poetic evocations of these fanciful world exhibitions. A "profane glow," he observed, "bathed" the commodity, eclectically arrayed in the marketplace, arcade, or *vitrine*. [15]

Taking her cue from Benjamin, the contemporary artist Judith Barry, whose work revolves around the visual dynamics of shopping, refers us back to the Greco-Roman tradition of exhibiting the spoils of war.[16] Her question "who possesses whom"—the conquered object or the conquered spectator/subject—is clearly relevant to the analysis of the ethnographic collection, but it is also implicit in surrealist montage. In the famous surrealist journal, *Documents* Clifford sees:

. . . the order of an unfinished collage rather than of a unified organism. Its images, in their equalizing gloss and distancing effect, present in the same plane a Châtelet show advertisement, a Hollywood movie clip, a Picasso, a Giacometti, a documentary photo from colonial New Caledonia, a newspaper clip, an Eskimo mask, an old master, a musical instrument—the world's iconography and cultural forms presented as evidence, or data. Evidence of what? Evidence, one can only say, of surprising, declassified cultural orders and of an expanded range of human artistic invention. This odd museum merely documents, juxtaposes, relativizes—a perverse collection.[17]

Though, in its display of heterogeneous objects, *Documents* clearly perverted the classificatory codes of the museological discourse, its order of things was not necessarily as arbitrary, as purely semiotic as Clifford seems to imply in this context. Picasso's paintings of African masks or Giacometti's "primitive" sculptural cages also appear (as Clifford is well aware) as self-conscious simulations of exotica rather than simply naive destablizations of taxonomy and its institutional mystifications. Commodification, with its cynical rites of replication and reproducibility, would seem to have installed itself at the very inception of surrealism.

In a catalogue essay for a show of contemporary art entitled "Damaged Goods," Hal Foster encourages us to see the scattered masks and cult figurines of avant-garde art and surrealism not as arbitrary signifiers but rather as magical commodities containing the repressed promise of a utopian cathexis between the work of art and society, between the artist and the viewer-consumer. "Was the (primitive object's) attraction," he queries, not, in part, its suggestiveness that (1) modern art might (re)claim a ritual function or cult value and (2) the modern artist, made marginal in the bureaucratic world of late capitalism, might (re)gain a shamanistic centrality to society?" Asserting that "(dis)agreeable objects," from the mask to the Duchampian ready-made, "demonstrated allegorically that the work of art in capitalist society cannot escape the status of a commodity," Foster, one may infer, wants to preclude the possibility of salvaging fetishism as a modern aesthetic.[18] But without falling into the trap of mystically reauthenticating fallen, alienated, neo-primitivism, we do perhaps find a place for modern fetishism in its artistic and theoretical definition of an ironic simulacrum. According to this line of reasoning, the fetish, in its relays between Africa and Europe, has escaped becoming altogether ossified, reified, or, as Foster has put it, "fetishized—its difference disavowed."

In the twentieth century, we are suggesting, the concept of fetishism (despite "damaging" criticism) has gone from being negatively to positively valorized in a number of ways. If Kant, Marx, and Freud gave it infelicitous ascriptions, then Georges Bataille and fellow members of the Collège de Sociologie, intent on shattering the complacencies of bourgeois civilization, recuperated fetishism as a form of transgressive idolatry. Strengthening its status as a perversion (more than the surrealists ever dared) Bataille and Michel Leiris transformed fetishism, along with a host of other de-repressed pathologies, into a

fig. 6

positive theoretical praxis. With his ironic invention of a spectator-fetishist whose "look" is displaced or implicated within a phobic narrative, Bataille, particularly in his *Histoire de l'oeil* (*Story of the Eye*), anticipated a number of postmodern narrators all perversely "scopic": Michel Tournier's *The Fetishist*, Patrick Süsskind's *Perfume*, Julian Barnes's *Flaubert's Parrot*, and Paul West's *Rat Man of Paris*, to mention just a few. In each of these novels fetishism is generated through the quest for trophies themselves ironically exposed as magical commodities.

Let us take as our most extended example Tournier's fetishist, depicted in the short story of the same title. Like a bloodhound, he tracks, expropriates and triumphantly worries his spoils—a lady's handkerchief, a bra, and best of all, a garter belt: "Je tenais mon trophée. . . . J'étais radieux. Je brandissais mon porte-jarretelles comme un Peau-Rouge son scalp de visage pâle"[19] ("I had my trophy. . . . I brandished my garter belt like a red Indian flaunting his paleface's scalp"). On the surface one fetish object is as good as another, but upon closer inspection we learn that these feminine undergarments function symbolically as mystical icons of capital. As *femmes chiffrées* (numbered women) appraised with all their measurements—bust, waist, hips—Tournier's mistresses, through a series of subtle permutations, are transformed into their masculine counterparts as money values: "les vieux billets déchirés, maculés, estropiés, mais surtout adoucis"[20] ("I was burning old, torn, dirty, mutilated bills—but the most important thing about them was that they had been softened").[21] Here the gender conversion from female to male fetish object parallels the conversion of sexual into commodity fetishes. If the fetishist performs a traditional Freudian substitution when he "deceives" his wife with another woman's bra ("Oui, quoi, je la trompais avec Francine par soutien-gorge interposé"[22] "Yes, all right, I *was* being unfaithful to her with Francine, with a bra as proxy"), he in effect, deceives the bra with a host of commodity idols: "Les combinaisons, les collants, les bas, les slips, les chemisettes, j'achetais, j'achetais, en moins de deux heures, plus un sou"[23] ("I bought, and bought, and in less than two hours we didn't have a sou left"). Finally, the fetishist's orgy of spending simulates the libidinal expenditure psychoanalytically associated with phallic substitution and points to paradigms of "economimesis" (cf. Derrida)[24] and meta-fetishism, or fetishism *en abyme* within Tournier's short story.

Throughout Tournier's fiction sexual desire is collapsed into the erotic *frisson* provoked by the commodity. In his recent novel *La Goutte d'or*, a title that refers to the Algerian quarter of Paris north of the Boulevard Montmartre, the attraction to material items subsumes the attraction to a real life object of desire. After a young Maghrebian named Idriss sells a polyethylene cast of his body to the Parisian department store Chez Tati, he is urged by one of the salesman to simulate himself as a commodity. The salesman states:

fig. 7

> *Et dans un mois une vingtaine d'Idriss, qui se ressembleront comme des frères jumeaux,*
> *vont peupler mes vitrines et mes étalages intérieurs. Alors, à ce propos, j'ai une idée que*
> *je voudrais vous soumettre. Voilà: supposez que vous appreniez à faire l'automate? On*

6.   7.

vous habille comme les autres mannequins, vos frères jumeaux. On vous maquille pour
que votre visage, vos cheveux, vos mains aient l'air faux, si vous voyez ce que je veux dire.
Et vous, raide comme un piquet dans la vitrine, vous accomplissez quelques gestes
anguleux et saccadés. Ça c'est déjà fait, notez-le bien. Le succès est assuré. Matin et soir,
c'est l'attroupement devant la vitrine.[25]

(And in a month's time twenty Idrisses, each resembling the other like twin brothers, will
populate my shop windows and display cases. And now, on this subject, I have an idea
that I'd like to try out on you. It goes like this: suppose you learn how to do the automaton
number? We'll dress you up like the other mannequins, your twin brothers. We'll make
you up so that your face, your hair, and your hands will seem fake, if you see what I mean.
And you, stiff as a rail in the window, you'll perform a few angular, spasmodic gestures.
It's been done before, mind you. A guaranteed success. From morning to night, it's a mob
scene in front of the store window.)

Transmogrified into a capitalist lure that magnetizes the rapacious "look" of the potential
customer, Idriss personifies the famous Marxist chiasmus of double alienation, by which
"people and things exchange semblances: social relations take on the character of object
relations, and commodities assume the active agency of people."[26]

Tournier's agents of commodification—postwar ogres, tourists, ad men, and
filmmakers—certainly discredit fetishism as a culturally constructed perversion and seem
to follow the received interpretation of fetishism as a negative effect of commodification.
But if we take the description of Idriss at one step removed, that is, as an illustration of the
ironic play of simulacra, we might begin to define a kind of critical fetishism; an aesthetic
of fetishization that reflexively exposes the commodity as an imposter value. In the mirror
reflection of a thousand identical department store mannequins, one can extract a political

critique of the alienated, colonized, North African self. In this sense, fetishism buys back its political redemption. Though Idriss may be prostituted, frozen, and reified, his dead stare (Medusa's head) gives back to consumer society the very alienation that consumer society has inflicted on him.

Let us examine for the moment this form of doubled fetishization and go on to explore what this may mean for contemporary aesthetic production. What creates the inherently doubled status of the fetish, to go back to Freudian theory, is the original paradigm of the ersatz phallus. Thus Freud writes in his 1927 essay on fetishism:

> When I now disclose that the fetish is a penis-substitute I shall certainly arouse disappointment; so I hasten to add that it is not a substitute for any chance penis, but for a particular quite special penis that had been extremely important in early childhood but was afterwards lost. That is to say: it should normally have been given up, but the purpose of the fetish precisely is to preserve it from being lost. To put it plainly: the fetish is a substitute for the woman's (mother's) phallus which the little boy once believed in and does not wish to forego—we know why. [27]

Freud's formulation employs, interestingly enough, a language of undecidability, as if by way of reinforcing the attitude of avowal and disavowal that he wishes to emphasize in his characterization of the fetishist. Caught between specular absences, Freud's fetishist seems to operate entirely in the realm of the simulacrum, generating a copy or surrogate phallus for an original that never was there in the first place. The Lacanian reformulation of this paradigm pictures the fetishist subject caught between "having" and "being" a maternal phallus that he or she can ultimately never possess, thus tersivergating between illusory mastery on the one hand and fantasms of lack or the permanently barred subject position on the other.

What emerges as particularly relevant here for an aesthetic critique is the uneasy mixture of credulity and disbelief that typifies the fetishist's attitude to the object-simulacrum.

Repressing the (hypothetically posited) existence of the maternal penis, he deflects his gaze to the nearest, most conveniently presented *cache-sexe*, as in the classic scenario of

fig. 8

boy and mother:

> Thus the foot or shoe owes its attraction as a fetish, or part of it, to the circumstance that the inquisitive boy used to peer up the woman's legs towards her genitals. Velvet and fur reproduce—as has long been suspected—the sight of the pubic hair which ought to have revealed the longed-for penis; the underlinen so often adopted as a fetish reproduces the scene of undressing, the last moment in which the woman could still be regarded as phallic. [28]

Expressions such as "ought to have revealed the longed-for penis" or "the last moment in which the woman could still be regarded as phallic" inject a subtle note of sympathy on the part of the analyst for the boy's suspension of disbelief. Freud's rhetoric, in other words, encourages us believe with the boy in the existence of an original phallic woman and in the viability of the fetish as a substitute for the female phallus that has been

8.

Emily Apter

9.

10.

fig. 9

lost. But such mistaken perceptions are only partially allowed to subsist. "It is not true that the child emerges from his experience of seeing the female parts with an unchanged belief in the woman having a phallus," Freud writes, "He retains this belief but he also gives it up."[29] In other words, though he knows that feet, underwear, and velvet constitute nothing but a false or simulated phallus, the Freudian fetishist continues to regard them as real *nonetheless*. (Octave Manoni's "je le sais bien mais quand même," "I know it but even so"). With true psychic ingenuity, or perhaps through the assistance of magical thinking, the fetishist manages to hold the simulated original in a state of ironic suspension adjacent to the real and the copy. As Freud would have it, this hexed state of mind is a compromise: "during the conflict between the deadweight of the unwelcome perception and the force of the opposite wish, a compromise is constructed."[30]

This characteristic of fetishization as specular mimesis, an ambiguous state that demystifies and falsifies at the same time or that reveals its own techniques of masquerade while putting into doubt any fixed referent, clearly has implications for the interpretation of all the arts. For now, and in conclusion, I would just like to speculate on several possible

11.

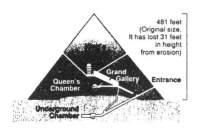

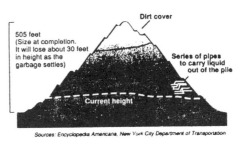

12.

architectural analogues. Here we might think about ways in which buildings function as ironic simulacra, that is to say, arouse conviction and skepticism at the same time.

The new, improved Harvard Square offers, perhaps, one possible mode of construing this architectural fetishization. The developers on Massachusetts Avenue have built "Harvard Square" on the site of "Harvard Square." Here the architecture attempts to authenticate the faux so as to "forget" a "real" that was already grounded in fiction. What we might call the "Harvard Square Fetish" exists as a memorial to a fantasmatically castrated Ivy League institution.

fig. 10

As Freud wrote:

In the world of psychical reality the woman still has a penis in spite of all, but this penis is no longer the same as it once was. Something else has taken its place, has been appointed its successor, so to speak, and now absorbs all the interest which formerly belonged to the penis. But this interest undergoes yet another very strong reinforcement, because the horror of castration sets up a sort of permanent memorial to itself by creating this substitute.[31]

fig. 11

A complementary and more felicitous example of a site's commemoration of architectural castration may be found in Antoine Grumbach's regional government center at Poitiers. An architect enamored of ruins, to the extent of building false foundations for a new town to the south of Paris, Grumbach was obliged to redesign his project for Poitiers when Roman remains were unexpectedly uncovered on his site. Fate, or the hidden power of the fetish perhaps, produced a building that "remembered" the architect, giving him ruins where he would have hoped to have found them; providing him with a fetish where he might otherwise have had to fabricate one for himself.

A more straightforward yet in some ways more understated form of fetishization might be associated with a particular approach to reading the city, to deciphering the ontologies of urban and suburban locales. Desublimating the ironic simulacra that lie hidden in certain place names, we would suddenly read the city otherwise: "city center" (the center has become the margin, nor did it ever exist); "senior citizens' home" (which represents the grotesque double of a real home, itself already ersatz); "supermarket" (a pun on "stock market"); "traffic artery" (already clogged and clotted); "art museum" (trying to capture a living culture that eludes enclosure within a cultural institution); "Venice, California" (American simulacrum of Europe); or "Disney World, Paris" (European simulacrum of America). In each of these examples the banal resemblance between the paradigm and its double engage us in a kind of permanently punned world view.

These paradigms of buildings that seem to act out their ersatz nature, winking so to speak, at the public as if to say that they are all too knowing about themselves as mystifying agents of commercial speculation, would then be one way of construing fetishism in architecture from the spectator's point of view. But perhaps, in the light of our short history of fetishism, another possibility arises, one more readily identified with the process of reification and monumentalization. Here I am less concerned with repeating the commonplace usage of fetishism as applied to monumental objects than with suggesting what is perhaps a less obvious model of reification, one applicable to the low life of objects. This would reverse the monumentalizing hierarchies implicit in, say, the obelisk as fetish by concentrating on the insignificant and the trivial as material for fetishization. In other words, one might shift the focus from that which is enduring, timeless, and culturally hegemonic to that which is ephemeral—the temporally marked effluvia of culture subject to the continuous erosion of time. Fetishization in this context would certainly reify, but in a way that would freeze the transient and preserve what is normally cast off.

Such a "Grub Street fetishism" might be further elaborated by exploring an approach to low-life or genre painting recently given a renewed theoretical status by Norman Bryson. In a recent study of still life and the space of the feminine Bryson retrieved Pliny's concept of *rhyparographos* to refer to the depiction of newly valorized inferior objects—trifles; ordinary, everyday commodities; degraded matter not dissimilar to what we earlier described as charms or small fetishes. Bryson noted that in its original frame of reference the word

had a distinctly pejorative connotation. When Pliny the Elder used the term in his *Natural History* he was referring to the painter Piraecicus, famed for his skill in rendering "barbers' shops and cobblers' stalls, asses, viands and the like, consequently receiving a Greek name meaning 'painter of sordid subjects'."[32]

Following Bryson, we might imagine that the genre *rhyparos* locates its equivalent in architecture somewhere in the margins of high design, in, for example, the creative use of junk (we think of Wallace Stevens's poem "Man on a Dump"). The jumble or tag sale, the storage room of disposable objects—objects that wear signs of abuse, love, chastisement, or neglect—would then be much like the underwear, money bills, and bric-a-brac of Tournier's fetishist. We might even extend this art of the small ware to a more general psycho-ecological aesthetic of production—the recuperation of waste, entailing geomorphic redistributions and revalorizations (as in Judith Barry's design for a primitive hut massed out of discarded coca-cola cans).

In this regard I was also interested to read in the *New York Times* of April 13, 1989   *fig. 12* that the plan for the Fresh Kills landfill in Staten Island was to construct, out of the waste of New York, a giant 50 million ton pyramid of detritus that by the year 2005 would have risen as high as the Statue of Liberty. The illustration carefully compared a section of this monument to and of waste with that of the Great Pyramid of Giza, demonstrating our ability to double it in size and volume. The city commissioner noted that one of the objectives of this exercise, besides disposing of the undisposable, was to remind New Yorkers of the important commodity waste had become. This example of postindustrial *rhyphophagy* (a term invented in the 1880s to refer to the perversion of "eating filth") happily combines the manifold dimensions of the theoretical fetish: as demystified commodity, as phallic (pyramidal) terror, and as desublimated simulacrum in which the subject sees itself mirrored in the *trompe l'oeil* of its own excrement.

Emily Apter

Footnotes

1.   Jean Baudrillard, *For a Critique of the Political Economy of the Sign*, trans. Charles Levin (St. Louis, MO: Telos Press, 1981), 90.
2.   Sigmund Freud, "Fetishism" (1927) in *Standard Edition* Vol. 21, 149.
3.   Karl Marx, *Capital: A Critique of Political Economy*, trans. by Samuel Moore and Edward Aveling, ed. Friedrich Engels (New York: The Modern Library, Random House, 1906), 81.
4.   Ibid., 82.
5.   Ibid., 83.
6.   W. J. T. Mitchell, *Iconology: Image, Text, Ideology* (Chicago and London: Chicago University Press, 1986), 81.
7.   Ibid., 163.
8.   Edward Tylor, *Primitive Culture*, Vol. II (New York: Brentano's, 1924), 143–159.
9.   Giorgio Agamben, *Stanze*, trad. Yves Hersant (Paris: Christian Bourgois, 1981), 69–71. See also Part II, Chapters I, II, III, V for discussion of fetishism in Marx and Baudelaire.
10.   Michel Leiris, *L'Afrique fantôme* (Paris: Gallimard, "Tel," 1981).
11.   William Pietz, "The Problem of the Fetish, I," *Res* 9 (Spring 1985), 6. I am deeply indebted to William Pietz's brilliant work on fetishism. Our discussions have nourished and influenced many of the arguments put forward in this essay. The above article, and its companion piece "The Problem of the Fetish, II," *Res* 13 (Spring 1987) offer an invaluable synthesis of fetishism's etymological ambiguities as well as its inner contradictions as a cross-disciplinary critical discourse.
12.   Pietz, "The Problem of the Fetish, I," 6–9, 14.
13.   Pietz, "The Problem of the Fetish, II," 45.
14.   James Clifford, "On Ethnographic Surrealism," *Comparative Studies in Society and History* 23, no. 4 (October 1981): 542.
15.   Walter Benjamin, Section on "Taste" in "Addendum to 'The Paris of the Second Empire in Baudelaire,'" *Charles Baudelaire: A Lyric Poet in the Era of High Capitalism*, trans. Harry Zohn (London: New Left Books, 1973), 105. Benjamin writes:
". . . mass production, which aims at turning out inexpensive commodities, must be bent upon disguising bad quality. . . . The more industry progresses, the more perfect are the imitations which it throws on the market. The commodity is bathed in a profane glow . . ."
In another section on fashion in "Grandville or the World Exhibitions" Benjamin associates fetishism with prostitution and a kind of pornography of death:
"Fashion prescribed the ritual by which the fetish Commodity wished to be worshipped, and Grandville extended the sway of fashion over the objects of daily use as much as over the cosmos. In pursuing it to its extremes, he revealed its nature. It stands in opposition to the organic. It prostitutes the living body to the inorganic world. In relation to the living it represents the rights of the corpse. Fetishism, which succumbs to the sex-appeal of the commodity recruits this to its service." (166)
16.   Judith Barry, "Dissenting Spaces," *Damaged Goods: Desire and the Economy of the Object* (Exhibition Catalogue) (New York: The New Museum of Contemporary Art, 1986), 49.
17.   Clifford, "Surrealism," 552.
18.   Hal Foster, "(Dis)agreeable Objects," *Damaged Goods*, 13.
19.   Michel Tournier, "Le fetichiste," *Le Coq de bruyere* (Paris: Gallimard, 1978), 298. For translations, see Barbara Wright, *The Fetishist* (Garden City, NY: Doubleday & Co., 1984).
20.   Ibid., 290.
21.   Tournier inadvertently raises the question of fetishism and gender when his fetishist classifies his objects of obsession according to criteria of sexual difference:
"Les femmes, c'est du linge fin, douillet, parfume. Les hommes, c'est un portefeuille gonfle de choses secretes et de billets de banque soyeux et odorants." ("Women are delicate, soft, perfumed lingerie. Men are a wallet swollen with secret things and silky, sweet-smelling bills.")
Ibid., 292.
22.   Ibid., 296.
23.   Ibid., 297.
24.   Jacques Derrida, "Economimesis," *Mimesis des articulations*, ed. Derrida et al. (Paris: Flammarion, 1975). Derrida evokes a mimetic (in the sense of "singerie") and infinitely specular chain of representations that refer in themselves to a libidinal economy of representation. See in particular p. 66–71.
25.   Michel Tournier, *La Goutte d'or* (Paris: Gallimard, 1985), 219–220. The translation that follows is my own.
26.   Marx as paraphrased by Foster, *Damaged Goods*, 13.
27.   Freud, "Fetishism," 203.
28.   Ibid., 201.
29.   Ibid. 200.
30.   Ibid.
31.   Ibid.
32.   Pliny the Elder, *Natural History* Vol. IX. Book XXXV, trans. H. Rackham (Cambridge, MA: Harvard University Press, 1952), 345.

Illustrations

1. G. G. de Clérambault, Photographic study of veiled Moroccan woman, from *La Passion des étoffes chez un neuro-psychiatre,* (Paris, 1981).
2. G. G. de Clérambault, Photographic study of veiled Moroccan woman, ibid.
3. Man Ray, *Slipper-spoon,* from André Breton, *L'amour fou* (Paris: Editions Gallimard, 1937), 48. Copyright A.D.A.G.P., Paris, V.A.G.A., New York, 1986.
4. Maurice Heine, Genealogical Tree of Perversions, from "Note sur un classement psycho-biologique des paresthésies sexuelles," *Minotaure* 3–4 (December 1933): 36.
5. Mrs. Pierre Loeb with her collection of modern and tribal works, Paris, 1929, from James Clifford, *The Predicament of Culture* (Cambridge, MA: Harvard University Press, 1988), 210. Albert Loeb Gallery, Paris.
6. *Man with Figurines,* from Paul Eluard, "Les plus belles cartes postales," *Minotaure* 3–4 (December 1933): 97.
7. *Veruschka,* Photograph by Holger Trülzch, from Michel Tournier, *Des clefs et des serrures* (Paris, 1979), 152.
8. *Boy with Mother,* from Paul Eluard, "Les plus belles cartes postales," 89.
9. *Au Musée Grevin,* 1959, Photograph by Pablo Volta, from André Breton, *Nadja* (Paris, 1964), 178.
10. *Harvard Square,* Cambridge, MA, postcard.
11. Antoine Grumbach, Direction Départementale de l'Equipement, Poitiers, France. Axonometric of Roman remains discovered during excavation of foundations. From Antoine Grumbach, "Les noces de l'architecture et de l'archéologie," *Monuments Historiques* 136 (December 1984), 55.
12. Diagram of Fresh Kills Garbage Pyramid compared to the Great Pyramid of Khufu (Cheops), from *New York Times,* 13 April, 1989. Copyright 1989 by The New York Times Company. Reprinted with permission.

TRACY BROWN

The Poem and the High-Heeled Shoe: Fetishization and Narrative

One of the most salutary influences of New Criticism is in the area of teaching poetry in the universities. The pervasive influence of New Criticism in the 30s, 40s and 50s has penetrated into the minds of many generations of students who are now exercising enormous influence in the academic world of literary studies.[1]—*J. N. Patnaik*

S ALUTARY OR NOT, the New Critics trained several generations of literary critics and general readers, in part through a series of popular and effective textbooks that, with their invisible, anonymous and authoritative "I's" of the textbook narrative, circulated both the teaching methodology and the critical ideology of New Criticism. The "fictional quality," the narratological aspects of the New Critical phenomenon are central to my argument; if we create fictions that tie together literature, reading, history, and ideology in order to work as readers and critics, then the story New Criticism told about literature is available for scrutiny as much as the next fiction. I'd like to explore the New Critical story with a special strategic tool, *another* narrative, the story of the fetish as told by Freud. Freud's story of the process of fetishization provides an arena in which to investigate the ways in which politics, desire, and denial collide not only in his own story and the New Critical story but in other contemporary narratives, namely in the fictions circulating in the current canon debate. The ways in which the characters in Freud's story fetishize objects like the high-heeled shoe parallel the way in which literature is fetishized for the New Critics, the way in which the canon and liberal arts education are fetishized for Bloom and his contingency, and the way in which that fetishized canon and that fetishized higher education refigure and are re-presented in the discourse of those participating in the debates about the canon and the academy. Only through understanding our collective history as critics can we choose to embrace or reject the influence which that history continues to have on our work as readers and thinkers. The strategies presented revolve around the use of fetish-theory as tool available for appropriation in interdisciplinary narratives.

According to the Freudian scenario, the fetish operates as a "screen-memory," hiding the true object of desire and/or repulsion from immediate view.[2] What is at stake behind all narratives is what resides behind the screen-memory, be it fear of the woman's

1.

body, fear of politics, fear of change, or fear of the consequences of living in a postmodern age. We have access to what lurks behind the screen constructed through the controlling project of fetishization because the *object* of that fear or desire remains persistent, haunting, refusing to stay silenced behind the screen—effectively demanding subject-hood. In this way exploring the idea of fetish can become literary and/or political strategy; further, the strategy can be appropriated to investigate all kinds of stories we tell ourselves. The New Criticism story offers an ideal site within which to explore the idea of fetish as theoretical strategy. Further, the way in which the New Critical agenda is now being reworked to justify conservative limits on ideas of sources of knowledge and participation in the liberal arts structure is stunning.

Freudian construction of what a "fetish" is can be understood in terms of the "story" of a skewed version of the castration complex, represented as psychological truth by Freud. The castration complex hinges, for Freud, on the sight of the female genitals. "Probably no human being is spared the fright of castration at the sight of the female genital," Freud writes. "Why some people become homosexual as a consequence of that impression, while others fend it off by creating a fetish, and the great majority surmount it, we are frankly not able to explain."[3] The main character in this story, the young boy, is simultaneously both horrified ("the greatest trauma of his life") *and* fascinated by the "lack" made visible in the sight of woman and immediately turns his gaze away.[4] His gaze is redirected-onto her lingerie, down to her boots, her high-heeled shoes and ah!—the birth of a fetish. Freud offers different versions of this story at various moments in his writings as he works out his ideas. Early on he gives weight to the workings of scopophilia in the process of fetishization:

> *In a number of cases of foot-fetishism it has been possible to show that the scopophilic*
> *instinct, seeking to reach its object (originally the genitals) from underneath, was*

brought to a halt in its pathway by prohibition and repression. For that reason it becomes attached to a fetish in the form of a foot or shoe, the female genitals (in accordance with the expectations of childhood) being imagined as male ones.[5]

In other words, Freud imagined the childhood expectation would be to see genitals like one's own genitals and further that that expectation would be so strong for the potential fetishist that the redirected gaze would imagine the female foot or shoe to be like the penis. Later, Freud writes of "other cases (wherein) the replacement of the object by a fetish is determined by a symbolic connection of thought, of which the person concerned is usually not conscious."[6] Freudian fetish then can be imagined as consisting of three parts: the subject whose gaze is redirected, the screen-memory or fetish object, and, importantly, what is behind the screen-memory: the origins of the entire fetishization project.

Several consistent themes emerge in Freud's stories of fetish. First and foremost, the main character or subject is always male. This male character possesses two instincts: the scopophilic instinct-desire as manifested in the gaze—and the intuitive ability to instantly "read" or interpret the sight of the female genitals as loaded with the threat of castration.[7] Further, the male gazes at an *object*, the woman, who receives the gaze. And finally, whether prohibition, repulsion, or fear thwart the gaze, the desire in this story must be redirected; the gaze refocuses on a non threatening object. The high-heeled shoe stands in for the woman, or more interestingly, the woman becomes "like" the man: her foot is reinterpreted, reimagined as a phallus. Rather than confronting what is different, the fetishist turns to another object, another reading of experience that he can control and with which he can identify. Freud wrote his story cognizant of its similarity to earlier narratives: "Such substitutes," he says of the fetishized objects, "are with some justice likened to the fetishes in which savages believe that their gods are embodied."[8] Freud's use of "symbolic connection" in the construction of fetish and his stress on women's bodies as the "natural" site of anxiety are doubly important for how they work in the New Critical story—the woman's body in both narratives can be metaphorically read as symbolic of repressed politics.

New Criticism grew out of a group of Southern poets and critics associated with Vanderbilt University in the 1920s. Self-named the Fugitives, they held the distinctly Southern agrarian and politically conservative view that only in a traditional, rural society like that of the antebellum South could human beings achieve mental and physical completeness.[9] Many of the Fugitives like John Crowe Ransom, Warren Tate, Robert Penn Warren, and Cleanth Brooks became associated with the New Criticism. Although they disagreed on other matters, the New Critics "were united in their emphasis on dealing with the text directly; they insisted that a work of art be considered as an autonomous whole, without regard to biographical, cultural, or social speculations."[10] The pervasive influence of New Criticism in the thirties, forties, and fifties translates into the presence of several generations of students, including myself, trained

to read and teach New Critically, stressing formal rather than political or historical considerations.

Although it may be possible to *ignore* the cultural, social, and political when considering or creating a work of art, those forces are at work. The fetishized object here then, is Literature with a capital L, which operates as a screen-memory to displace those forces from view or consideration. The New Critics are subjects who redirect their gaze from the political and social issues of their time in order to conceive of literature as a controllable realm of truth and beauty.

The New Critics present their story to their readers not just in critical essays but in a series of popular and effective textbooks. I would argue that reading in *An Approach to Literature*, authored by Cleanth Brooks, John Purser, and Robert Penn Warren and first published in 1936 and revised in the 1950s and 1960s, the text written by the New Critics, the introductory essays, in effect the "margins" of that text reveals a disturbing sexism in the presentation of the New Critical ideology.[11] This sexism is not symptomatic but endemic to the critical methodology. In other words, the attitude toward women in *An Approach* is ideologically tied up with the New Critical approach toward literature. The place delegated to women in this text reflects a general attitude toward the place of politics, culture, history-indeed, anything not reflecting the white, male viewpoint of the authors. In the essays preceding the major sections of the textbook the connections between the story of fetish and the New Critic's overprivileging of the place of Literature begin to unravel.

The book's section on Fiction begins with an introduction naturally headed "What is Fiction?" Uncomfortable as a postmodern critic might be with answering such a question, Brooks, Purser, and Warren answer easily: "Fiction, like the essay, play, poem, sermon, or philosophical treatise, is the projection of the author's view of life."[12] The authors extend their discussion to explain why people read fiction:

> It may be added that the impulse that leads people to read fiction is fundamentally the same as the impulse that leads to its creation. The reader wants to enter more fully and understandingly into life, and therefore turns to the controlled images of life the writer has prepared. Fiction extends his experience of life, and at the same time feeds his fundamental curiosity about life and its meaning. (p. 9)

According to this scenario if, as readers, we have the *desire* to enter more "fully and understandingly into life," that desire is not directed into a physical or emotional engagement with life in the "real" sense (assuming here a division between fictional and real worlds) but rather into the "controlled *images* of life" created by the author. No distinction is made between the experience one would gain from participation in the world of the text versus the physical world outside the reading experience: "Fiction extends his experience of life."

Parallels to the Freudian story emerge. Naturally the main character is male, whether we take that main character to be reader, author, or New Critic. Again, we have

Tracy Brown

instinctive drives, here figured as "fundamental impulses"—fundamental impulses to read and write and a fundamental curiosity about life and its meaning. Again that desire is redirected, toward controllable and controlled images. Controllable, of course, in that the author's "controlled images," which exist to fulfill the desire for experience, are the ones chosen and framed by the New Critics for attention in this textbook. Rather than entering life, the reader redirects that desire to controlled images; rather than dealing directly with female sexuality, the fetishist turns to another experience, one that he can control.

Why the intersection of literature at the juncture between subject and world? John Crowe Ransom writes on this point in his 1933 essay "Forms and Citizens": "The aesthetic forms are a technique of restraint, not of efficiency. They do not butter our bread, and they delay the eating of it. They stand between the individual and his natural object and impose a check upon his action."[13] For Ransom, like Freud, the individual—the protagonist of his story—is male, and the "natural object" is female. Ransom illustrates his point by explaining the ways in which a man many approach a woman:

> He may approach directly, and then his behavior is to seize her as quickly as possible. No inhibitions are supposed to have kept the cave-man or pirate, or any of the other admired figures of a great age when life was "in the raw," from taking this severely logical course. If our hero, however, does not propose for himself the character of the savage, or of animal, but the quaint one of "gentleman," then he has the fixed code of his gens to remember, and then he is stopped from seizing her, he must approach her with ceremony, and pay her a fastidious courtship. We conclude not that the desire is abandoned, but that it will take a circuitous road and become a romance.[14]

Here literature—poetry, fiction, drama—intervenes, as do manners, between the savage and the woman, between the reader and the world, to redirect the gaze, the impulse, the desire. Ransom's choice of the word "ceremony" as all that prevents the social man from raping the woman implicates him. Form is the only boundary between the "savage" and the "social man"—they have in common the desire to act directly upon the woman. Without literature and manners, the fetishist would gaze on in horror, the reader would directly experience the world, and the savage would rape the woman. Form hides the crudeness of the desire. The "form," in fact the fetishization of form, prevents the chaos of desire undirected and misdirected.

Not just any form will do, for elsewhere the text makes this distinction:

> There is the enjoyment found in Hamlet, and that found in a western. The two kinds of enjoyment have certain elements in common, but there are important differences. The aim of this book is to indicate, little by little, some of these differences. The reading of good literature does give pleasure—a very keen pleasure—but there is no use in saying that Hamlet gives a "higher" pleasure than the western if we cannot indicate, however fumblingly, that higher and keener pleasure is. (p. 1)

The stress in *An Approach* is on a certain cultured distancing that seems to allow for experience without getting one's hands "dirty" (the shoe rather than the genitals?). If pleasure comes from the experience of fulfilled desires, a very definite sort of pleasure ensues from the fulfillment of desires that have been redirected carefully away from the low, dull pleasure of the western to the keener, higher pleasure of Shakespeare. Thus, form redefines the savage into a social man, the uneducated student into a discerning reader, and the woman of the Ransom scenario into—what? Ransom again: "But the woman, contemplated under restraint, becomes a person and an aesthetic object; therefore a richer object."[15]

Again, Ransom's choice of the word "object" gives him away. If only under the contemplative gaze of a man she becomes both a person—a subject, one presumes—*and* an aesthetic object, who or what was she previously? Returning to the pages of *An Approach*, what *she* is is a dead body. Importantly, I would argue that the recurrent display of a dead woman's body in the pages of this introductory textbook reveals the ways in

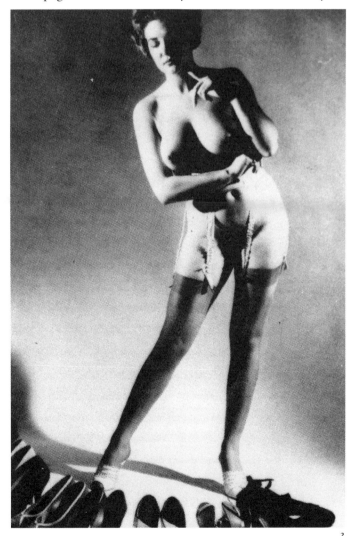

2.

which the presence behind the screen-memory, literally and symbolically women, denied by the fetishized object—Literature—demands attention and demands subjecthood.

The general introduction to *An Approach to Literature* chooses to use the murder of a young woman as the "arbitrary" example from which to show what is and what is not literature. "Suppose that we take an incident. A man murders a girl with whom he is in love."(p. 1) This woman's body, Porphyria *Blank* as she is named, is available for consumption on every page of the introduction. To illustrate the New Critical tenets on literature, she is described in a coroner's report, in a newspaper account, in a sentimental literary version, and in a Robert Browning poem, the last offered to the refined reader, here termed the "college man." Examining the handling of the woman's body reveals the ways in which New Critical assumptions about experience and fiction, however unconscious, are neither as innocuous nor as apolitical as they desire to present them. The overdetermined presence of dead and battered women in the New Critical narrative highlights the presence of the screen-memory. Thus the New Critical story begins: "Suppose that we take an incident." Random incident, chance choice on the part of Brooks, Purser, and Warren? No. In fact, the incident comes directly from the Browning poem "Porphyria's Lover," which serves as the introduction's central example of "what good literature is." The entire essay is constructed to showcase the Browning poem, but the reader cannot anticipate that. Step by step, the authors set the stage for their presentation. "How do the literary accounts differ from the practical and factual accounts?" is answered by the autopsy surgeon's report, which describes the marks of strangulation on the body:

> Death occurred from the effects of asphyxia, cerebral anemia, and shock. The victim's hair was used for the constricting ligature. Local marks of the ligature were really discernible: there was some abrasion and a slight ecchymosis in the skin. But I found no obvious lesions in the blood vessels of the neck. Cyanosis of the head was very slight and there were no pronounced hemorrhaged in the galea of the scalp. (p. 2)

The legal indictment that follows offers another male voice describing the death of "one Porphyria Blank by strangulation" and, interestingly, gives the killer the name John Doe—the representative tag for any and all anonymous males. (p. 3) The newspaper account follows, in which it is implicitly suggested that the woman is responsible for her own murder because she thwarted her lover's desire:

> Doe was found holding the body in his arms, and appeared to be in a stupor, his only reply to repeated questioning being, "I killed her because I loved her." According to members of the Blank family, Doe had paid attentions to Miss Blank for the last several months, though it was strenuously denied that his regard for Miss Blank was returned. Miss Blank's engagement to Mr. Roger Weston was announced last month. (p. 3)

The murderer *loved* Porphyria, the family *strenuously* tries to deny that she encouraged his love. The framework of the classic blame-the-victim scenario begins to be

articulated in the newspaper account, and is accentuated when the authors write under the guise of a woman in what they term the "sob sister's story," another account of the murder that they label poor literature. Meanwhile, the authors point out that "all three of these accounts [the autopsy report, the legal indictment, and the newspaper account] are concerned with facts and *only* with facts" (p. 3).

The editors of the textbook plead innocent by asserting that this section of the introduction illustrates facts and only facts. However, the lurid choice of a murdered woman as a random basis for discussions of what literature is and is not raises issues of violence, sexism, voyeurism, and politics precisely excluded from the New Critical program for reading. *An Approach* does acknowledge the usefulness of the non literary text: "Moreover, almost any poem or story or play based on the incident would probably leave out facts which the man of practical interests would want to know: e.g. the address of the house where the dead girl lived or a technical description of the state of the dead girl's lungs and of the bruises on her throat." (p. 3)

A distinction is set up between "the man of practical interests" who would voyeuristically want to know about the bruises on the girl's throat and the refined college man whose controlled voyeurism would push him to choose Browning poetry. Again, *form* intercedes for the civilized; the savage covets the woman. The fetishized object is Literature, operating as a screen-memory for "direct engagement with life," which might entail an acknowledgment of the place of politics, history, and biography. The references to a more direct engagement with life-murdering women, reading the paper for evidence about a corpse's bruises, seem disturbingly predicated on violence.

In the violence that erupts from the introduction, pedagogy and ideology collide. The woman student reader of *An Approach* who has been repeatedly confronted with this image of a murdered woman about her own age (the newspaper account says twenty-one) *is* provided with another female role model. However, *the* female writer portrayed here is the "sob sister," author of a story that is, in the New Critic's words, only "in intention, literature." (p. 3) In the sob sister's account, the now familiar dead woman's body is "beautiful and peaceful in death, her scarlet lips slightly parted as though whispering a caress to her lover." (p. 3) Further, the sob sister sentimentally portrays the murderer as one deserving of our sympathy because he cannot be with the one he loves: "And this is the irony of fate! The very greatness of his love made him strangle her. Separated as they were by wealth, social position, and all that implies, it was only in death that they could be united. Who are we to pass judgement on such a love? (p. 4) Porphyria's murder is secondary to the romanticism of the idea of killing for love.

Compared to Browning's poem, the sob sister's work is "much more general, and consequently, much more crude"(p. 4) The woman writer fails because she cannot tell us "the direct perception, the picture . . . when the man looked into Porphyria's eyes and asked himself how his happiness with her could be preserved." (p. 4) Ironically, the woman

writer they portray in the introduction is themselves in drag, trying to fulfill their own equation between what poor literature is and what a woman writer would write. The anthology will not seriously contest this portrayal of a woman writer because even the revised edition of 1964 still contains 283 entries by men to sixteen by women—11 of those 16 written by Emily Dickinson. Finally, the sob sister idealizes and glorifies the image of the dead female body. The New Critics end up allowing a glimpse behind the screen of their own fetish construction. This woman author acts as a vehicle for the editors to fulfill their own prophecies—she writes poorly, sentimentally and without conviction on a subject worthy of rage. The pedagogical implications for women student readers and authors are disheartening, as the textbook offers no real alternatives besides ineffectuality or silence.

Finally, when presenting the centerpiece poem "Porphyria's Lover," the "I" that has judged, indicted, and observed the murder and the murderer in the various voices of judge, coroner and reporter is embodied in the narrative voice. The poem is written in the first person; in other words, the murderer speaks. The student reader unconsciously conflates the "I" of the poem with the reader's own "I" and effectively gets to "murder" Porphyria Blank. Only the voice of high literature is permitted to draw the reader in, to convey the immediacy of the first person: "I found/ A thing to do, and all her hair/In one yellow string I wound/ Three times her little throat around/ And strangled her." (p. 4) This is the literature promised, capable of satisfying that desire redirected away from engagement with life. Browning's poem is celebrated because in "his relatively short piece of writing the poet has given us more penetration into the psychology of the murderer than the writer of the sob story has." (p. 7) The reader is invited to participate in the process of fetishization by killing through poetic form. What needs killing or repressing is not only woman's body or women's writing but what they metaphorically represent. The continual reappearance of the woman in the narrative, bruised, dead, and incompetent, calls attention to the inadequate repression occurring.

The Porphyria scenario is used repeatedly to frame each new section in *An Approach*: fiction, poetry, discursive prose and drama. The dramatic version of Porphyria's murder which heads off the drama section, includes such lines as this question from the murderer: "Can you feel guilty, Porphyria?" (p. 614) Furthermore, the violence against women theme persists throughout *An Approach to Literature*. For example, literary terms like suspense or action are illustrated violently. Here, action is explained: "Let us consider an example. Looking from the window of a moving train at night we see, under a streetlamp, a man strike a woman with his fist, so that she falls to the pavement." (p. 11) The savage acts upon the woman, but when Literature is fetishized we act upon the woman through a ceremony, the ceremony of form, of art. The poet does not hit the woman with a fist but represents the violence with language. In fact, to represent violence in terms of aesthetics—to use the murder of a woman to illustrate literary terms—abrogating critical responsibility, is in itself a violent act. Evidence of the violence of the act of fetishizing literature keeps seeping back through the narrative in the overdetermined presence of the literary violence. The violence running beneath the image of cool, cultured Southern gentlemen living the literary life, silencing the black and/or woman writer or student, ignoring the issues of race in the South in order to represent the region literarily—as a bucolic, agrarian place where man's true nature can be realized—allows the cultured surface of the New Critical text to splinter under close reading. I would not argue that violence should not be allowed depiction but that the persistent recourse to violent imagery in order to depict, to teach what literature is, demands attention. Language mediates the experience, but the screen-memory cannot contain the issues that it is asked to contain-the presence not only of women but of the forces of culture, history, politics, and biography that New Criticism seeks fervently to deny as relevant to the study of literature. The very choice of "random example" and the overuse of that example points to something off-key, felt in the presence of the dead female body strewn across the pages of *An Approach to Literature.* Her body works as a metaphor for all that is beyond the screen-memory and illuminates what is actually being fetishized here—literature.

In the New Critical text, Literature is fetishized, the traditional and male-authored forms of poetry and of fiction are the vehicles for redirected desire. The object of fetishization presents itself as overread, overdetermined. The murdered female body insists from behind the apparatus of the screen that the politics, culture, and social forces of the New Critical ideology be marked. Certainly the New Critics are time-bound by their own history and politics, and my very act of deconstructing their pedagogical tools is a move I can make only from within my own historical moment. For my contemporary Allan Bloom, the information and energy is there to make that move, yet somehow he makes the same gesture as the New Critics to fetishize not only literature but all of the liberal arts as the form that can transmit Truth, at the expense of cultural and political reality. Obviously the process of fetishizing something is not necessarily negative and can be seen to work in many narratives. However, a fetish is a substitute and may stand in at the expense of silencing real people and real lives.

The Closing of the American Mind, with its near religious subtitle, *How Higher Education Has Failed Democracy and Impoverished the Souls of Today's Students*, acts as a "blueprint for the revival of a conservative system of education utterly out of date with contemporary cultural and political realities."[16] Bloom's book, along with E. D. Hirsch's *Cultural Literacy,* has served as a right-wing cornerstone in the extended national controversy over higher education. I would argue that the impassioned prose surrounding the debate is an overdetermined sign pointing to the construction of a fetish.

Bloom glorifies the Great Books program in a manner reminiscent of the New Critical position toward definitions of what is literary; Bloom is more explicit in his refusal to acknowledge the elitist politics behind his position:

Of course, the only serious solution is the one that is almost universally rejected: the good old Great Books approach, in which a liberal education means reading certain generally recognized classic texts, just reading them, letting them dictate what the questions are and the method of approaching them—not forcing them into categories we make up, not treating them as historical products, but trying to read them as their authors wished them to be read.[17]

The control so coveted by the New Critics makes a comeback here with the "certain generally recognized classic texts" to be read according to the questions they dictate, outside of systems of desire, history, and theory and of questions readers might bring to the text. The classic texts are the category of Literature. Bloom designates the liberal arts university as the ideal sanctuary where literature can be understood by a very specific cultured student. Bloom acknowledges, parallel to the New Critics acknowledgment of the place of the nonliterary, the presence of "other" types of students:

There are other kinds of students whom circumstances of one sort or another prevent from having the freedom to pursue a liberal arts education. They have their own needs and may very well have very different characters from those I describe here. My sample, whatever its limits, has the advantage of concentrating on those who are most likely to take advantage of a liberal education and to have the greatest moral and intellectual effect on the nation.[18]

Bloom fetishizes the liberal arts students of privilege in the name of some kind of national goal of perfection. Ignoring issues that must be part of his horizon as a university professor-issues of race, affirmative action, class, and sexism—Bloom separates students into the categories of "us" and "them." "*They* have their own needs," he writes, essentially saying that only those students who ask his questions are worthy of higher education. Stridently unwilling to accept diversity, Bloom defends his stance by yet again invoking loyalty to his fetish object—the potential of a truly liberated liberal arts experience—one free from the distractions of the stranger: "The reason for the non-Western closedness, or ethnocentrism, is clear. Men must love and be loyal to their families and their peoples in order to preserve them . . . A very great narrowness is not incompatible with the health of an individual or a people, whereas with great openness it is hard to avoid decomposition."[19] His overreading of the university as the site where the "truths" that protect our culture and the correct "values" can be learned from the great books and where culture, history, and politics should be denied admittance, alerts us to the process of fetishization taking place. Aligned with the New Critical reader who desires engagement with life and turns to the controlled image of Art, Bloom indicts the university for failing to make that same move. Saul Bellow concurs: "Liberal democracy in its generosity made (the university an island of intellectual freedom), but by consenting to play an active or a positive, a participatory role in society, the university had become inundated and saturated with the backflow of society's problems."[20]

If indeed Bloom makes a fetish object of the Liberal Arts University, what is at stake behind the screen-memory? The characters that Bloom, the New Critics, and Freud create in order to immediately deny by writing them out take revenge on their authors by pushing through the screen. A story told or written becomes immediately a story released from its author's stronghold, always available for rereading by readers who come to the text from different historical positions. Those readers may, in fact, be the readers denied presence and subjecthood in the story, hidden behind the screen-memory. Just as the presence of the dead women in *An Approach* alerts us to the process of fetishization, the readers behind the screen-memory may refuse to stay invisible, to remain repressed. Attending to those voices allows us access to the possible reasons for the original fetishization of the liberal arts experience, the canon, and literature, at the pointed expense of political and social realities. *Multi-Cultural Literacy: The Opening of the American Mind* is a collection of essays that explicitly takes on the Bloom-Hirsch contingency. Compare Bloom's words to those of Guillermo Gomez-Pena, a visual artist living in San Diego:

> *The borders either expand or are shot full of holes. Cultures and languages mutually invade one another. The demographic facts are staggering: The Middle East and Black Africa are already in Europe and Latin America's heart now beats in the U.S. . . . In this context, concepts like "high culture," "ethnic purity," "cultural identity," "Beauty," and "fine arts" are absurdities and anachronisms. Like it or not, we are attending the funeral of modernity and the birth of a new culture.*[21]

3.

Gomez-Pena's euphoric embrace of cultural relativism, of the influx of multicultural voices, highlights the way in which Bloom so energetically seeks to deny their relevance. Gomez-Pena's radical understanding of the culture's revolutionary status shows up Bloom's position for what it is: at risk. The ivory tower is neither ivory nor a tower anymore; the tower's symbolic connations—white, phallic, austere, and privileged—are being challenged on every front. Blacks, feminists, scholars studying popular culture, Afro-American Studies, gay studies, etc. etc. . . . force reinterpretation, reorganization, and removal of the traditional liberal arts university, from it's curriculum to it's student body to it's faculty hiring procedures. Freud nicely wraps up the connection between fetishization and a reactionary like Bloom:

> *What happened, therefore, was that the boy refused to take cognizance of the fact of his having perceived that a woman does not possess a penis. No, that could not be true: for if a woman had been castrated, then his own possession of a penis was in danger; and against that there rose in rebellion the portion of his narcissism which Nature has, as a precaution, attached to that particular organ. In life a grown man may experience a similar panic when the cry goes up that Throne and Altar are in danger, and similar illogical consequences will ensue.*[22]

On the other hand, Gomez-Pena's euphoric conviction that the change is already upon us, that we are witnessing the death of the old and the birth of the new accounts neither for what may be unsettling to both the left and right about the cultural relativism implicit in much poststructuralist and postmodernist thought nor for the real life presence of people like Bloom who have power, control committees and publish well circulated books. The fetishized objects that act as substitutes, as Freud points out, are like the fetishes that "savages" believed embodied their gods. The key here seems to be less that we should live without gods than that we should be aware of how our gods work to reveal or repress our desires and denials, particularly when we recognize that our critical work takes place in a world with other people, other agendas, and other readings.

In the case of Freud, his own theory work may be the place to look for his own redirected desires and fears. The fetish story as presented by Freud codes women's sexuality as dangerous and different. He finds safety in identifying it as absence. Feminism rewrites Freud, refusing to remain behind the screen-memory. Bloom's fetishization of the liberal arts experience, his careful glorification of the university as an arena capable of disconnection from society, points to a similar process of fetishization in his narrative. The canon as locus of truth and timeless value is a fetishized canon. When that canon is refigured by those who discover the presence of oppressive political agenda behind the fetishized object, their anti-canons run the same risk of fetishization if the canons are forced to contain *all* that has been repressed and oppressed out of the original. For the New Critics, literature became fetishized at the expense of acknowledging the politics, history, and culture of reading and writing and doing critical work.

The project of fetishization: the repression, prohibition, or deliberate reprojecting of the gaze that signifies desire onto an object capable of containing and controlling that denial, those thwarted desires, and the concomitant erection of a screen—the fetish object—to conceal what is really at work, is a useful story. Freud offers up a way, by introducing the term screen-memory, for the reader to immediately turn back to the story he has just finished telling—the story of fetish—to search for the presence of a screen and what is behind it. As readers, writers, and critics desiring not to abrogate political responsibility, we must read the labels on the ideological equivalents of our lingerie and our high-heeled shoes to see where they come from, where they were constructed, and for which sociopolitical conditions they stand.

Footnotes

1. J. N. Patnaik, *The Aesthetics of New Criticism* (Atlantic Highlands, NJ: Humanities, 1983), 83.
2. Sigmund Freud, "Three Essays on Sexuality," *The Standard Edition of the Complete Psychological Works of Sigmund Freud*, trans. James Strachey (London: Hogarth, 1981), vol. 7:154.
3. Ibid.
4. Freud, "An Outline of Psycho-Analysis," *The Standard Edition* 23:203.
5. Freud, "Three Essays on Sexuality," *The Standard Edition* 7:155.
6. Ibid.
7. Freud, "Leonardo Da Vinci and a Memory of His Childhood," *The Standard Edition* 11:96.
8. Freud, "Three Essays on Sexuality," *The Standard Edition* 7:153.
9. *Benet's Reader's Encyclopedia*, 3d ed (New York: Harper and Rowe, 1987), 812.
10. Ibid., 689.
11. James Sosnoski examines the margins of these textbooks in his working paper "*The Magisterus Implicatus* as an Institutionalized Authority Figure: Rereading the History of New Criticism," The GRIP Report: Second Draft, vol. 1.
12. Cleanth Brooks, John Thibaut Purser, and Robert Penn Warren, *An Approach to Literature*, 4th ed. (New York: Appleton-Century Crofts, 1964), 9. All future references to this text will be made in the text.
13. John Crowe Ransom, "Forms and Citizens" in *Selected Essays of John Crowe Ransom*, ed. Thomas Daniel Young and John Hindle (Baton Rouge: Louisiana State Press, 1984), 60.
14. Ibid., 61–62.
15. Ibid., 62.
16. *The Graywolf Annual Five: Multi-Cultural Literacy*, ed. Rick Simonson and Scott Walker (Saint Paul: Graywolf Press, 1987), introduction, n.p.
17. Allan Bloom, *The Closing of the American Mind* (New York: Simon and Schuster, 1987), 344.
18. Ibid., 22.
19. Ibid.
20. Saul Bellow, introduction to *The Closing of the American Mind*, 18.
21. Guillermo Gomez-Pena, "Documented/Undocumented," in *The Graywolf Annual Five: Multi-Cultural Literacy*, 130.
22. Freud, "Fetishism," in *The Standard Edition* 21:153.

Illustrations

1. From left to right: Allen Tate, Merrill Moore, Robert Penn Warren, John Crowe Ransom, and Donald Davidson in Nashville in May 1956. Courtesy *The Nashville Tennessean*.
2. From *Bazaar*, no. 10, ca. 1960, Copenhagen, Denmark. Reprinted with permission from *Caught Looking: Feminism, Pornography & Censorship*, edited by Kate Ellis. Copyright 1986 by The Real Comet Press, Seattle.
3. Still from *The Lady from Shanghai*, directed by Orson Welles.

R. E. SOMOL

Les Liaisons Dangereuses, or *My Mother the House*

fig. 1

fig. 2

EFORE DISCUSSING THE RELATIONSHIP of the mother's body to architecture in the work of Robert Venturi, it seems necessary to begin by marking the occasion of an anniversary, one which will help set the primal scene, a glimpse of architecture in the bedroom. Fifteen years ago at Princeton, in April 1974, Manfredo Tafuri presented "L'Architecture dans le Boudoir: The Language of Criticism and the Criticism of Language." That same year Tafuri's essay was published in *Oppositions 3*, an issue that also included a review of Venturi's *Learning from Las Vegas*, as well as a "vignette" by Rem Koolhaas that would form part of *Delirious New York*—a book that provided its own image of the architectural primal scene.

Tafuri's title alludes to René Magritte's *La Philosophie dans le boudoir* (1947), a painting that depicts the hybridization of articles of clothing in a woman's dressing room, suggesting both the animation of objects and the petrification of life. Although Tafuri does not make much of his allusion, these lively supplements should haunt the following discussion and its images. Together with the two framing aspects of Tafuri's paper (the date and title), its two subjects—namely, a consideration of the architectural neo-avantgarde and the role of criticism—will complete the four points to be pursued in this mapping of architecture and the fetish, in this celebration of the crystal anniversary of Tafuri's paper. Briefly, I propose to concentrate on the architectural experiments of a particular historical moment—between 1966 and 1974—and outline their connection to a critique of postwar modernism. The success of this critique has ultimately led to a refetishization of architecture, one which suggests that Tafuri's critical method—based on the model of the surgeon—remains relevant but must be redefined to contest contemporary configurations of theory and practice.

Rather than trying to impose a specific meaning of "fetish" onto architecture, I'll begin by leaving it in a general sense: the projection onto an architectural object of

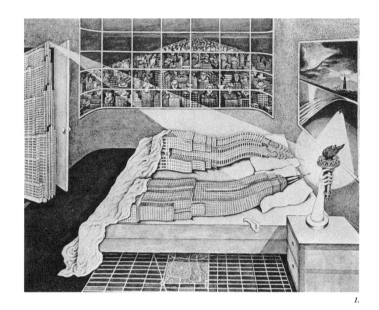

1.

2.

a value or meaning extrinsic to it, or the investment of a desire in it that could be said to be displaced from somewhere else. This most basic sense of the fetish consists of granting an object a power and mystery it lacks or is feared to lack. This assignment may arise first in a certain kind of animistic or anthropomorphic discourse that purports to disclose "the secret life of buildings," investigate "what a brick wants to be," or even discover what is "in the nature of the materials." Often, this attitude maintains that a building "speaks." Together these theories and practices drape an "aura" around the architectural object, an aura—and authority—that it becomes the task of the professional faithful to produce, maintain, and explicate.

From this preliminary definition one can see why Tafuri's project requires casting the critic in the role of the surgeon. For Tafuri, the historian must cut into the body of architecture and not perpetuate or promote the illusory powers or magic of particular practitioners. As he says in his 1974 essay, "wishing to discover the tricks of a magician, it is often better to observe him from behind the scenes rather than continue to stare at him from a seat in the audience."[1] Tafuri's critical opposition of surgeon to magician repeats the contrast Walter Benjamin develops with regard to the cameraman and painter:

> *The surgeon represents the polar opposite of the magician. The magician heals a sick person by laying on of hands; the surgeon cuts into the patient's body. The magician maintains the natural distance between the patient and himself. . . . The surgeon does exactly the reverse; he greatly diminishes the distance between himself and the patient by penetrating into the patient's body. . . . Magician and surgeon compare to painter and cameraman. The painter maintains in his work a natural distance from reality, the cameraman penetrates deeply into its web. There is a tremendous difference between the pictures they obtain. That of the painter is a total one, that of the cameraman consists of multiple fragments which are assembled under a new law.*[2]

For Benjamin, the cameraman—whose function is predicted by the historical avant-garde—undermines the aura created by the traditional painter as well as the institutions of authority and ownership affiliated with it. This defetishization is intimately related to the "tactile" eclipse of distance Benjamin sees as accompanying the rise of the mass media (as well as the rise of the masses). As will be seen later, this discursive opposition of distance to proximity—which on the level of audience reception corresponds to contemplation versus participation or testing—emerges as one of the primary organizing principles in the debate over modernism in the late sixties and early seventies. For now, it is enough to note that Tafuri fully identifies the role of the critic with that of the cameraman-surgeon. As he writes: "The critical act will consist of a recomposition of the fragments once they are historicized: in their 'remontage.'"[3]

3.

In contrast to Tafuri's surgeon, Vincent Scully represents the architectural magician *par excellence*. In the same year as Tafuri's essay, Scully publishes *The Shingle Style Today, or The Historian's Revenge*, a book whose two-part title almost too literally demonstrates Derrida's observation that "the desire for attribution is a desire for appropriation"[4]—what Scully identifies or restitutes to a particular tradition he ultimately returns to himself. In his discussion of Venturi's Trubek and Wislocki Houses Scully's anthropomorphic projection reaches dazzling, even Icarian, heights:

fig. 3

> The two new houses stand side by side on a bluff above the bay at Pocomo, with every variety of old and new shingled house, from 1973 to 1986, to be found not far away. But these two stand very much alone, and their tall vertical stance gives each of them a special quality as a person; we can empathize with them as the embodiment of sentient beings like ourselves. . . . [T]hey turn like two bodies slightly toward each other as if in conversation. Here semiology approaches its essential, which is the action of people talking to each other: not now gods, . . . but common creatures dwindled to modest human scale. . . . The windows of each house are in tension with those of the other, a family in response and withdrawal. The conversation is difficult . . . the smaller more slender house withdraws from the other broader one. How lonely each seems, as Americans have somehow always felt themselves to be. How stiff their backs. . . . For these new houses on archaic Nantucket there is no planting, and the height of the block foundation is as it has to be, unadorned. How hard is our American present, it seems to say; how threatened, beneath the superficial affluence, with instant poverty on a national scale.[5]

Scully, of course, is the great American architectural ventriloquist. In this instance, he gets two vacation houses on a secluded island for the relatively wealthy to speak about national poverty. For Scully these structures come alive, like the garments in Magritte's boudoir, to converse as heroic individuals in a situation not dissimilar to the architectural pillow talk parodied in Vriesendorp's illustration.[6] Scully deploys a magical language of criticism to celebrate and cast an aura around these now fetish houses. But the architectural neo-avantgarde of this period—of which Venturi is one

R. E. Somol

manifestation—has always displayed an ambiguous relation to the problem of architecture and its fetishization.

Whatever their differences, the various neo-avantgardes confront the problem of modernism's reconstruction and institutionalization in postwar America as high culture. Of course, this transformation was already implicit in the 1932 formalization of the modern movement as the "International Style."[7] The ultimate symbolic detachment of the modernist social and political program occurred in 1949 with the film version of the modern architect as individualist hero in Ayn Rand's *The Fountainhead*. In general, the modernist aesthetic was recast in postwar America to serve two ends: to express symbolically the public realm and to serve the various needs of the private. Reconstruction modernism thus succeeded to the extent that it reexpressed the twin halves of the postwar liberal consensus, and this split program accounts for both the monumental (largely urban) and regional (largely suburban) forms that the second generation modernists adopted in postwar America. While much of Venturi's work can be seen as contesting the unconscious expressionism (or external symbolism) associated with monumental urbanism, Peter Eisenman's early projects focus on a critique of the unreflective functionalism (or internal structure) that appeared most clearly in the domestic architecture of suburban regionalism.

On one level, architects like Venturi and Eisenman came to reenact and repossess strategies initially developed by the European avant-garde movements of the teens and twenties against a modernism that had become the new form of high culture. Given the different problems they initially identify within reconstruction modernism, Venturi exhibits a surrealist interest in the everyday landscape and popular iconography while Eisenman pursues a formalist analysis of the structure of architectural language. This rediscovery of surrealist and formalist strategies was not unique to these architects, of course, but can be seen as the primary characteristic for a variety of contemporary artistic experiments, from pop to minimalism. The confluence of these projects across professional disciplines and artistic practices in the late sixties and early seventies also engendered a related historiography. This new historical scholarship reexamined the monolithic characterization of "Modernism" that flourished after the war, and identified an often opposed element suppressed within it—that of the historical avant-garde—whose project of transforming personal and social relations and dislocating bourgeois institutions of high culture had never been an aspect of American modernism.

In addition to returning to earlier avant-garde paradigms, the new cultural vanguards were forced to confront the conditions of a fully realized consumer society. Whenever possible they began to employ the insights and techniques gained from the mass media that, more powerfully, were already demonstrating the obsolescence of the hierarchies and distinctions built into the postwar alignment of welfare liberalism and high modernism. In this respect, photography and film emerge as the precondition for the neo-avantgarde's

54

critique of postwar, "high" modernism. These media, previously threats to the presence of architectural experience, to the sincerity and authenticity of a Kahn or Mies, are located by Venturi and Eisenman at the center of architectural discourse. Despite the differences between them, both architects challenge reconstruction modernism by giving priority to the architectural supplement (the "secondary" graphic, textual, photographic, and plastic media traditionally used to represent built form), and thus turn their "actual" buildings into the sign or trace of architecture. Here architecture becomes conceived and built from the point of view of its reproducibility. In this way, they contest the fetishization of postwar architecture—typified, for example, by the sculptural "duck" of Saarinen's zoomorphic TWA building—by dematerializing the object of architecture. From today's vantage point, however, it appears that this dematerialization ultimately condemned architecture to a higher level of fetishization as it began to be framed by a new market that provided more powerful substitute exhibition and publication values.

As this brief survey begins to suggest, the neo-avantgarde's ambiguous relationship to the fetish derives from the new professional role that these practitioners adopt, that of the architect-critic. This new role—new, that is, by the extent to which it allows these architects to predetermine and coopt the reception and discussion of their work—emerges as another aspect of the neo-avantgarde's erosion of the postwar institution of architecture. By confessing or abdicating their professional function as producers, these architects assume the task of re-producer: critic, theorist, advertiser. This is precisely the situation Tafuri described as early as 1968 and against which he began to define the "pure critic" as surgeon. As the design equivalent of the inside trader, the neo-avantgarde architect-critics both analyze and invest in the fetish. More specifically, they collapse the opposed aspects of surgeon and magician, and this new condition—symptomatic of the dual crisis of liberal and modernist representation—is registered throughout their practice.

First, in the projects of the neo-avantgarde there is no humanist space from which to evaluate and appreciate architectural form (a space common to classical as well as high modernist works), and one is forced into the roles of critic and performer, subject and object, simultaneously. Just as individual authorship has lost its position and explanatory power through the abdication of the architect's traditional role and the discourse of autonomous reproduction, the privileged status of ownership is equally abandoned. In these dwellings the owner is never at home. Consequently, the architectural object and inhabitant must seek their identity together; they are extensions of one another allowing neither priority. This is the inversion—or perhaps complete realization—of Richard Neutra's postwar "bio-realism," the recognition that the "humanization of the machine" called for by Joseph Hudnut and Lewis Mumford releases its suppressed other: the mechanization of the human. Implicit in this neo-avantgarde production is that the *machine a habiter* does not serve or represent man with deferential

4.

5.

6.

fig. 4

fig. 5

ease and transparence, but that man and the machine are indissolvable. This incarnation of the mechanical, despite the denials and repressions by critics of various persuasions, appears in the first "postmodern house" when Venturi places his mother in precisely the position that, in an International Style building, would be occupied by the car.

Venturi has been named "the father of postmodern architecture"[8] largely on the basis of his writings and early work, especially the house he completed for his mother in 1964. As Stanislaus von Moos has observed, the Vanna Venturi house "has come to play a role in postmodern architecture that is comparable to that played by Le Corbusier's Villa Savoye in the International Style."[9] For Denise Scott Brown, this house "has become an icon of Postmodernism and is now part of history."[10] It is almost exclusively on the basis of one photograph, endlessly reproduced, that this house has been marked as the origin of postmodernism and Venturi's paternity.

For Vincent Scully, the Vanna Venturi house (or, more specifically, the *photograph* of the house) signals the return to humanism after the excessive reductivism of the International Style. As Scully writes,

> *Venturi gave us one central image when he replaced the heroic male figure of Vitruvian tradition, the "Man of Perfect Proportions," with the photograph of his mother sitting in the entrance of their house, right in the center of the Platonic circle and square. In this, he let all the air out of the macho image of the universe and invoked the fundamentally liberationist character of his generation.*[11]

Scully and other critics believe that Venturi's work illustrates a renewed balance between nature and culture as well as a concern for physical context, human scale, and

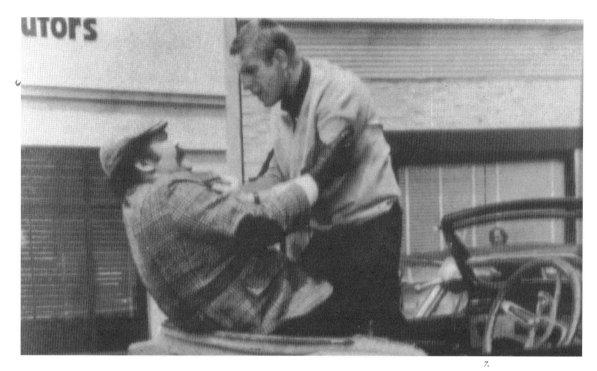

7.

narrative symbolism.[12] It is exactly because Venturi challenges reconstruction modernism, however, that his projects—despite the humanist faith of Scully and others—represent a complete realization of the goals of the historical avant-garde. Here, an over emphasis on formal differences obstructs more significant continuities. If one attends to Rollin R. La France's canonical photograph of the Vanna Venturi house closely enough, as to Neville's drawings in *The Draughtsman's Contract*, a pattern of clues emerge: to a plot, a murder, an illegitimate paternity, the hidden agenda of modernism now recovered by the neo-avantgarde.

It is one of the most famous images in recent architectural history, the founding act of American postmoderism: Venturi's mother sits dead center at the vanishing point—framed successively by the portico, the house, and the photograph itself—and presides at the threshold between the places of nature (the lawn) and the machine (the driveway). Although there is an open book on her lap, she is looking up as if she has just been interrupted. In the first framed space there are potted flowers to the left and the sun passes diagonally across the top of her head from left to right. Outside, the trees are bare; it is possibly early spring, perhaps late March. What is being staged here, appropriately enough, is an Annunciation scene, and the house is merely the domestic architectural setting requisite for this elaborate tableaux vivant. But what is being announced is more than simply the "birth" of Venturi and postmodernism.

fig. 6

The Vanna Venturi house announces the theme of the mechanical extension of the body, a dangerous liaison between the "machine-for-living" and the body of the architect's mother. In the immaculate conception of Robert Venturi there is a genealogical

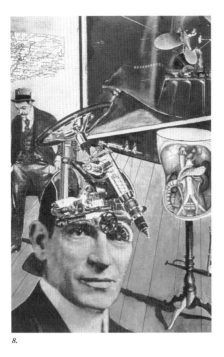

8.

9.

fig. 7

inversion, for it is the son who reproduces the mother in the mechanical womb of his house, a house that most resembles a child's drawing with its stylized elements of pitched roof, overscaled chimney and entranceway, and linear ("drawn on") ornamentation. Moreover, as seen earlier, Venturi places his mother in the place of the car in the same year as the short-lived television series *My Mother the Car*, a sitcom whose protagonist (Jerry Van Dyke) realizes that his mother has been reincarnated as a talking 1928 Porter.[13] As Venturi will do again in the Lieb House and in *Learning From Las Vegas*, he identifies the human form with the machine. Andreas Huyssen provides an accurate account of this desire in his analysis of Fritz Lang's *Metropolis*, in which Dr. Rotwang creates a machine-woman double of the virgin Maria.

> In the drive toward ever greater technological domination of nature, Metropolis'
> master-engineer must attempt to create woman, a being which, according to the
> male's view, resists technologization by its very "nature." . . . By creating a female
> android, Rotwang fulfills the male phantasm of a creation without mother; but
> more than that, he produces not just any natural life, but woman herself, the epitome
> of nature. The nature/culture split seems healed. The most complete technologization of
> nature appears as re-naturalization, as a progress back to nature.[14]

Rather than the "return to nature" posited by humanists like Scully, Venturi's work more accurately continues and fulfills the historical avant-garde's vision of the unification of man and machine, most literally represented in the combined subjects of photomontage, but also present in the reflections of constructivism, futurism, dada, and surrealism. Venturi's mother is a parody of Hudnut's "post-modern owner,"[15] a mere extension of "her" post-modern house, and the thin facades inspired by

billboards and movie screens are comical surrogate walls whose futile struggle to separate "mass ecstasies" from "inner experiences" serves only to reveal their ultimate identity. This "pop" sensibility was already prefigured by Richard Hamilton's *Just What Is it That Makes Today's Homes So Different, So Appealing?*, which appeared in the 1956 exhibition "This is Tomorrow" and which represents one of the first examples of the postwar recovery of the historical avant-garde's technique of photomontage.

      Unlike the productions of Berlin dada—for example, Raoul Hausmann's *Tatlin at Home* or Hannah Hoch's version of the woman-car centaur, *Pretty Maiden* (both 1920)—Hamilton has no need to graft the machine onto the human directly since the advances of postwar consumer culture have made that image redundant. Instead, Hamilton's orbital living room illustrates the complete satellization of reality, where the terrestrial body's only connection to its natural home (the earth, the "real") is through the communication networks of the mass media. This is the final frontier of the modernists' *existenz minimum*, where the inhabitant's survival depends entirely on the support systems and networks of information provided by the postmodern house.

fig. 10

fig. 8

fig. 9

10.

Like the photograph of the Vanna Venturi house, Hamilton's photomontage recalls the Annunciation, where the strongman-Gabriel presents the impregnating word ("POP") to the seated vamp-virgin crowned by a floating hat-halo and surrounded by the classic iconographic elements (books on knee, plant, candle). Finally, the passage of light from the window down toward the woman, presumably disseminated from the movie marquee (hence, a cinematic rather than a solar seed), is suggested in the diagonal white area above the lampshade-car logo. Here, too, Hamilton suggests his own equivalence between woman and car by visually aligning the combined Ford logo and lampshade with the woman who sports a lampshade-like hat.

Rather than emphasizing cuts and fissures between images as did the historical avant-garde (perhaps representing the not yet fully realized nature of the man-machine hybrid in the 1920s), Hamilton's seamless image is located in the "naturalistic" and total space of Renaissance perspective which provides an overall unity to the elements. This unity, of course, is modeled on the photograph and, more specifically, the film, where discrete images are mounted and juxtaposed to give the illusion of continuity.[16] Here, the exaggerated use of an earth-bound and subject-oriented perspective system in an environment that is undecidably extraterrestrial or subterranean (below grade)— in either case an atmosphere devoid of horizon line—signifies the desperate loss of unmediated presence and reality, the impossibility for private moments of self-identity and sufficiency. Through reproductive and testing technologies reduced in scale to the "privacy of one's home," the domestic scene becomes the site for the self-production and consumption of pornographic souvenirs or incriminating evidence.[17] In part, the neo-avantgarde documents as the largely established condition of postindustrial consumer society what the historical avant-garde could only project as its program-matic suspension of classical boundaries (e.g., between art and life, man and technol ogy, private and public, culture and nature, reason and desire, representation and reality).

It is against this condition of advanced capitalism that the postwar humanists and reconstruction modernists redefined the self, nature, and originality to be the true touchstones of modernism.[18] Overall, the postwar discourse of reconstruction moder-nism—and this can be seen to unite a variety of diverse thinkers from Clement Greenberg, Colin Rowe, and the New Critics to Michael Fried, Stanley Cavell, and Daniel Bell—came to rely on the possibility of "distance" and boundary maintenance, the faith that traditional political (liberal) and aesthetic (high modernist) representation could work, and that there was no need for theatrical participation, no need to take "it"—politics or art—to the street. As an object of contemplation, the modernist work of art for Fried is a fully integral essence which is equally manifest at every moment. In contrast to his favored, purely optical modernism, Fried posits Tony Smith's description

of driving on an abandoned highway with its onrush of perspective as the kind of experience of endlessness that Fried disapproves of in a theatrical art like minimalism.

Once again, from this perspective of the passenger, the man in the machine, one can see how far the neo-avantgarde architect-critics have traveled from their contemporary defenders of high modernism. In fact, almost all of Venturi's projects can be understood through this dialectic between the flat, frontal perspective with fixed distance and the theatrically exaggerated one-point perspective—the suction (and seduction) of the strip—and the increasingly rapid alternation and oscillation between them.[19] While the timeless character of the Venturi house composition recalls the mode of the painter, the "found image" of the Las Vegas billboard and highway corresponds *fig. 11* to the temporally fragmented practice of the cinematic cameraman—or again, magician and surgeon. Significantly, Venturi organizes this dialectic in terms of the woman's body, the poles announced through the classic figures of virgin and vamp, Vanna and Tanya.[20]

The always present desire to collapse these female roles, and the perspective systems associated with them, is most clearly achieved in the Lieb House, where the attractively tanned younger mother seated at the entrance of her house combines the *fig. 12* aspects of Vanna and Tanya. In the photograph taken from the upstairs living area of *fig. 13* the Lieb House, the owner/mother is targeted between the crosshairs of the semi-circular window that serves as the overscaled aperture for this box-house with its closing shutter. When framed by the entranceways to their houses, from the perspective of the

11.

12.

13.

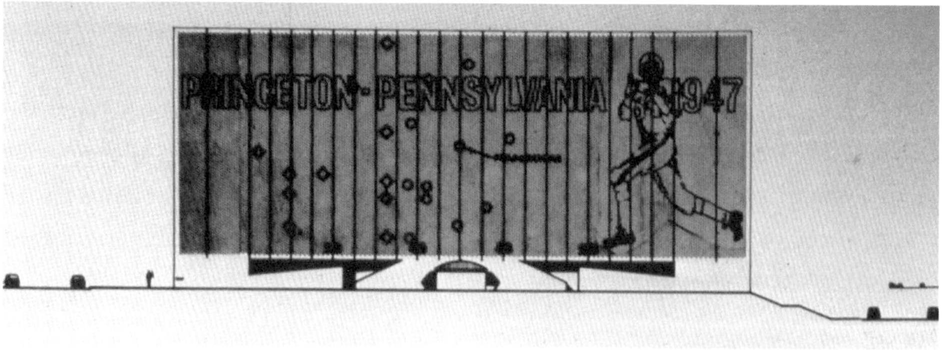

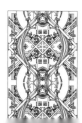

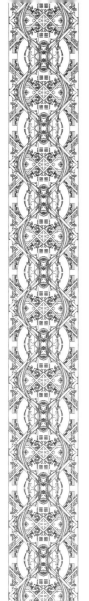

14.

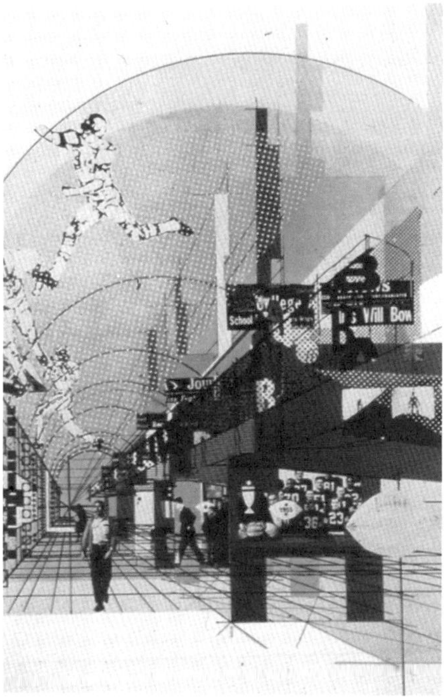

15.

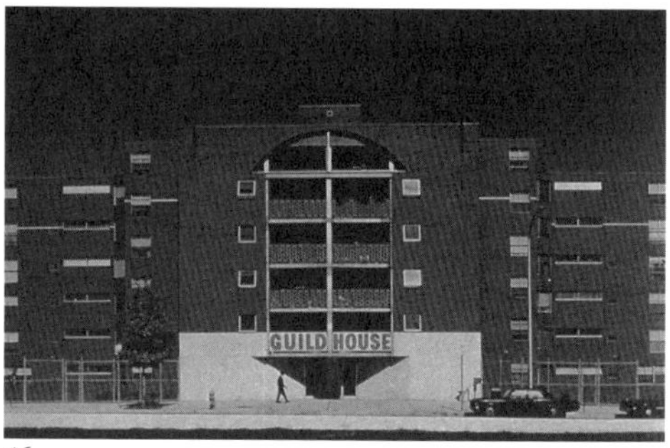

16.

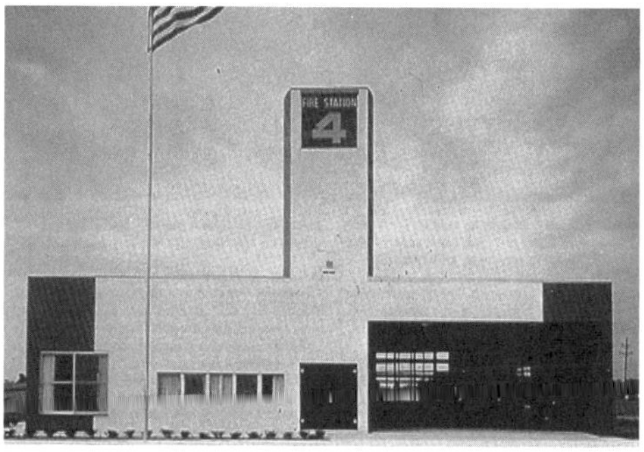

17.

driveway or street, Mrs. Venturi and Mrs. Lieb assume the position of the car; when reproduced through (and by) the inside of her house, Judy Lieb is attached to the car (specifically, as its rear wheel). Here, there is a doubling of the once sovereign and primary owner/mother as she is reproduced both in the belly of the house (inside) and through its eye (outside). This dual representation of Mrs. Lieb, who is identified alternatively with the house and the car, begins to suggest the related aesthetic and political agenda of the late-sixties neo-avantgarde. At its most general, this program desires either to overcome the immanence/transcendence dichotomy, or at least to register the impossibility of reconciling or balancing this fundamental contradiction through the illusory techniques of postwar liberalism and modernism.

In substituting his mother for the car, and the functionless TV antenna for the Madonna that he had originally planned to place atop the Guild House, Venturi identifies the female body with the technologies of transportation and communication, technologies largely responsible for the erosion of architecture's traditional stability. Implicitly, Venturi's woman—particularly as the phallic mother—is a threat to architecture. Significantly, the only figures visible in both the interior and exterior photographs of the Lieb House are Judy Lieb and the number "9", which appears in supergraphics to the left of the front door and is miniaturized and reproduced in negative on the couch throw pillow. In each instance the relative size of the maternal body and the sign are identical; the mother-seductress and symbol of information have dissolved the architecture.[21]

The most complete realization of this process, and the architectural equivalent to Hamilton's orbital communications living room, appears in Venturi's "billdingboard" entry for the National Football Hall of Fame Competition. Once more, this project combines a flat, frontal elevation that reexpresses its graphic representation with a highly illusory and theatrical one-point perspective. On the outside, the front elevation resembles a billboard or drive-in movie screen. After entering through the bottom of this screen the visitor is surrounded—and the architecture is covered—by a multimedia assault, depicted by Venturi in a collage in which object, viewer, and setting become indistinguishable. As described by Venturi: "Movies . . . are almost all over. They spill over the surfaces, essentially independent of the architectural forms they smother . . . . The message dominates the space."[22] Apparently, the only contradiction here is merely architectural, between the flat external facade and the interior vaulted space of the shed that sits behind it. The boundary between inside and out can only filter and separate (now largely defunct) architectural or spatial differences. As in Hamilton's living room, where the inhabitants are completely engulfed by information and communications technology, Venturi's walls are completely permeable to the images of the mass media. The wall that Venturi exaggerates to serve as a record of the conflict between inside and outside cannot maintain itself against the media that it would imitate; it is only the nostalgic and ironic reminder of a time when such an extravagance could provide security. Like the work of Hamilton and others, Venturi's architecture is primarily about boundaries (or frames) and their dissolution.

In the "cardboard architecture" that the neo-avantgarde produce, structure is conceived and built from the point of view of its reproduction. Venturi suggests this reduction or inversion of architecture in *Complexity and Contradiction in Architecture* when he discusses the operation of the wall.

> *Since the inside is different from the outside, the wall—the point of change--becomes an architectural event. Architecture occurs at the meeting of interior and exterior forces of use and space. . . . Architecture as the wall between the inside and the outside becomes the spatial record of this resolution and its drama.*[23]

For the modernists, "space" had been the primary product of architecture which was created by the stretched skin of the enclosing wall. In Venturi's analysis the wall,

fig. 14

fig. 15

that which was secondary, becomes primary since the flat *record* of spatial contradiction emerges as the significant concern. In fact, this secondary "event" (the wall) *is* architecture, which for Venturi means part photographic record and part dramatic *tableaux vivant*, thus confirming the importance of the front entrance and the body positioned there. The habit of applying supergraphics to number or label his structures can now be seen to derive from his various reflections on architecture as document. This also explains the fact that, regardless of photographer, the exterior treatment of his buildings invariably produces an "objective," schematic or diagrammatic image. The photographs are taken head-on so that the architecture is flat, flush with the image surface, and almost fills the frame, suggesting an identity between building and photograph.[24] Of course, this problem of the "wall"—and the larger issues associated with it—was of great concern to a number of architects in this period, perhaps most memorably figured in the wall houses of John Hejduk.

fig. 16

fig. 17

In commenting on the Bye House, Tafuri provides an instructive analysis of Hejduk's project: "Once again, and this time explicitly, Hejduk relies on the movie screen, which also serves as a painter's canvas for a spatial 'counter-relief.'"[25] Almost unconsciously Tafuri hits upon the collapsed aspects of cameraman and painter present within neo-avantgarde production. This is exactly the same configuration developed by Venturi in *Complexity and Contradiction* when he describes the wall as "spatial record" (photographic document) and "drama" (narrative painting). The passion to combine these poles occurs in a variety of neo-avantgarde practices and is by no means limited to architecture. In fact, the clearest example of the attempt to unite cameraman and painter, surgeon and magician, appears in the contemporaneous work of the photorealists who would project a photographic slide onto a canvas and airbrush the image onto the surface.

fig. 18

fig. 19

In the work of Richard Estes the two dominant points of view reiterate those of Venturi—e.g., the flat, layered storefront of *Double Self-Portrait*, and the extreme one-point perspective of *Bus Reflections*. In addition to a radical symmetry and pervasive doubling of images, Estes's work appears motivated by the same desperate passion to overcome the dichotomy of representation and abstraction, inside and outside, here and there, *da* and *fort*. This last aspect begins to clarify Venturi's pervasive use of the mother figure, since the *fort-da* game, with its continual movement of loss and reunion, derives originally from the separation of the child from its mother's body. Apparently, Estes's reflective canvases are about the mirror stage in more ways than one. In this work, however, the loss is not merely recorded, but also covered in a complex way, and the resulting object finally emerges as a substitute. In Estes's method, the fugitive, photographic image is rendered permanent and auratic again, capable—against the hopes of Benjamin—of being owned and authored. A surgical, mechanical procedure is finally returned to the realm of magic. The twofold result of this is the revival of the

aura and the art object as fetish. This leads to the suspicion that the once critical products of the neo-avantgarde, capable of undermining the more obvious fetishization of reconstruction modernism, have become enchanted—were probably always enchanted—at a higher level. From this observation I want to conclude with a more speculative consideration of current critical practice.

Recently, there has been a powerful backlash against theory, a return to disciplinary rigor, of which the architectural concern with "making it" is only one manifestation. In the *New York Times Book Review* a few months ago, one born-again, straitlaced academic from the University of Chicago characterized contemporary critical initiatives as "miniskirts of the mind"[26]—which seems as close as the neo-conservatives can come to understanding philosophy in the boudoir. Meanwhile, support for interdisciplinary research and collaborative experiments has begun to be curtailed as there has been a reinvestment in the objects and languages of traditional expertise.

Against these trends, and in recognition of the fifteenth anniversary of Tafuri's essay, it is necessary to expand and modify his critical model of the surgeon. That model has become inadequate, in its pure form, precisely because of the combined role of the

18.

19.

magician-surgeon in practice. We can now begin to understand the shift from the late-sixties, when some members of the profession abandoned the values and practices established under reconstruction modernism, to today, when the result of that confession has returned—via the object—a renewed authority and power to these same architects. Apparently the disappearance and dematerialization of architecture twenty years ago was just a trick, and it has been made to reappear with great applause in venues like the Museum of Modern Art. This trajectory has been fully confirmed by the generation of theorists who have come of age in the past few years only to announce the end of theory. The circle is now complete with the investment in the object itself of a total criticality, with the marginalization of the critical and theoretical role.

To contest this absorption or circumscription of criticism, I propose two new models, two fictional paradigms, for Tafuri's critical surgeon. The first is William Burroughs's Dr. Benway. The scene is an operating theatre filled with students, whom Benway is addressing:

> *Now, boys, you won't see this operation performed very often and there's a reason for that . . . . You see it has absolutely no medical value. No one knows what the purpose of it originally was or if it had a purpose at all. Personally I think it was a pure artistic creation from the beginning. Just as a bullfighter with his skill and knowledge extricates himself from danger he himself has invoked, so in this operation the surgeon deliberately endangers his patient, and then, with incredible speed and celerity, rescues him from death at the last possible split second.* [27]

fig. 20

For Benway, the surgical operation becomes an art of performance. The second figure to be offered is Dr. Van Meegeren from Peter Greenaway's *A Zed and Two Noughts* (ZOO).

In a typically stylized and structurally symmetrical scenario, with its insistence on the agency of the letter and the plural, *Zed* involves twin zoologists, Oswald and

20.

Oliver Deuce, whose wives die in a freak auto accident. In their patascientific quest for the "reason" behind this accident, Oswald and Oliver become involved with the driver of the car, Alba Bewick, who through the course of the film losses her legs, gives birth to twins (uncertainly fathered by either Oswald or Oliver), and commits suicide (as do the two "noughts," Oswald and Oliver, by the film's end). In one way *Zed* poses its own version of the question, "what happens when you cross a woman with an automobile?" Although ostensibly the result of her car crash, the amputation of Alba's legs has more to do with the desire of her surgeon, Van Meegeren, who seems to specialize in removing limbs and replacing them with detachable prosthetic devices. Like his infamous namesake, Van Meegeren is obsessed with Vermeer, and he comes to see and remake Alba as a seventeenth century portrait. Once on Van Meegeren's procrustean operating table, surrounded by waist-up reproductions of Vermeer women, this fertile mother figure is cut to fit the frame and her legs, naturally, must go. As Alba says, she has become a guinea pig "for medical experiments and art theory." This film, then, emerges as one source for the operation performed on Mrs. Venturi which, if (un)successful, has left Scully without a leg to stand on.

Just as Benway and his procedure provide an allegorical substitute for Burroughs and his "cut-up" technique, so too Van Meegeren is one stand-in for Greenaway himself, who is a painter as well as a film director. In *Zed*, Van Meegeren takes great care in photographing his female companion and accomplice--who invariably appears in a red feathered hat—in settings meticulously modelled after those in paintings by Vermeer. In addition to one scene that perfectly reproduces Vermeer's masterpiece *The Art of Painting*, *Zed* also contains an ironic allusion to the *Girl in a Red Hat*, a small canvas in the National Gallery in Washington that many experts now consider to be a master forgery—thus Greenaway wittily engages in copying a copy. Van Meegeren and Greenaway are equally "forgers" of Vermeer, as well as cutters and suturers of bodies, and both occupy the now combined role of surgeon-magician. (In this regard, Van Meegeren's medical specialty can also be seen as the classic magician's trick of sawing a woman in two.[28]) But it is important to notice that Greenaway inverses the practice of a photorealist like Estes, by photographing scenes taken from paintings rather than painting photographic projections. In other words, unlike Estes, he travels the road of magician to end up as surgeon. (And in this, it seems to make all the difference in the world whether one moves from cameraman to painter or painter to cameraman.[29])

To summarize, this essay has endeavored to mime Tafuri's article, since the problems and concerns it raises remain relevant, while at the same time historicizing his particular solution. I, too, have examined the neo-avantgarde—most fully in the case of Robert Venturi—but, like Tafuri's treatment, this subject has been employed largely as a way of outlining a certain style of criticism, one which is other than that of some of the more recent "post-neo-avantgarde" critics.

R. E. Somol

In order to reinvigorate the figure of the surgeon I have attempted to adopt the techniques and procedures of Burroughs and Greenaway—which correspond to those of their fictional doubles, the surgeons Benway and Van Meegeren. This approach rejects the kind of schizophrenic, Janus-faced aspect of current criticism that initially overlays a supra-rational methodological system on architecture only to conclude with an evaluative leap of faith.[30] As Dr. Benway complains, "All the skill is going out of surgery. . . . All the know-how and make-do." By putting magic at the service of surgery, rather than vice versa, it is possible to put the "make-do" back into criticism. As in Greenaway's films, one manner of approaching this project is to seize arbitrary fragments and push coincidences into a seductive assemblage that upsets both the formal and substantive coherence assured by the guardians of reality, both of "language" and the "object."[31] This is one way to (re)imagine and (dis)figure "the language of criticism and the criticism of language."

Finally, one implication of examining Venturi has been to challenge a common strategy that conveniently dismisses Scully and Venturi on the same grounds and fails to recognize that the former constructs his professional ego, his consistent vision of a unified liberal-humanism, only through the mirrors of the latter. Not only does splitting them turn the magical aura against itself, thus diffracting Scully's humanist projection, but it also provides a more sophisticated picture of the conditions and situation of the American neo-avantgarde. While this does not represent any attempt to "save" Venturi, it does suggest the extent to which criticism has been expended by the early-seventies advertising campaign of the "white v. grey" wager. This capture leads to the suspicion that, in discussing the question of "architecture and the fetish," the problem is not primarily with particular objects, but with a system of relations, a system in which the house always wins, where the certainty of two noughts ("OO," or double zero) is masked by the illusion of chance. Today, the fetish in architecture (as elsewhere) multiplies through a faith in the code itself, in a network of differences, in the possibility of choice. The opposition of Venturi or Krier to Eisenman, or Jahn to Tschumi, serves only to cover the fairly widespread fear that there is really no difference, that building itself may not matter in those ideological terms any more, and that this is all part of the same economy of knowledge and power, the same confidence game.[32]

So, to celebrate the fifteenth anniversary of Tafuri's paper, I offer an arbitrary and unnecessary surgery, not life giving, but life threatening. While not producing death itself, it may stimulate a small one, the pleasure accompanying the possibility that our objects and contexts can become wholly other, different even from the dreams of those who would try to concretize and formalize a new canon of otherness. This is a criticism that plays with the fetishes of other(nes)s, that reuses the supplements—the detachable parts—that are imposed on us, and makes of them counter-fetishes or voodoo dolls. It schemes to venture the constantly shifting frames of architecture, its doubles, rather than torture its forms. In place of "making it," it desires "making do." Getting by between work.

Footnotes

1. Manfredo Tafuri, "*L'Architecture dans le Boudoir*: The Language of Criticism and the Criticism of Language," *Oppositions* (Cambridge, MA) 3 (May 1974): 57.

2. Walter Benjamin, "The Work of Art in the Age of Mechanical Reproduction," *Illuminations*, translated by Harry Zohn (New York: Shocken Books, 1969), 233–234.

3. Manfredo Tafuri, "The Historical Project," *The Sphere and the Labyrinth* (Cambridge, MA: MIT Press, 1987)

4. Jacques Derrida, "Restitutions of the Truth in Pointing," *The Truth in Painting* (Chicago, IL: University of Chicago Press, 1987), 260. Derrida remarks later, "Silence makes the expert speak," 314.

5. Vincent Scully, *The Shingle Style Today or the Historians Revenge* (New York: George Braziller, 1974), 34–36. Recently, Scully has invoked a more ornithological pedigree for these houses: "The porches which face the splendid view across the upper reaches of Nantucket Harbor are as sharply drawn as the beaks of birds, and the two houses together stand alertly on their bluff, turning slightly toward each other like, on the one hand, Greek temples, or, on the other, seabirds themselves." From the revised edition of *American Architecture and Urbanism* (New York: Henry Holt and Company, 1988), 258. In the space of fourteen years "sentient beings like ourselves" have inexplicably become birds, perhaps due to a "violent unexplained event" (VUE) like the one documented by Peter Greenaway in *The Falls* (1980) which engendered as identical transformation from man to bird.

6. As the following argument will suggest, Venturi's buildings are more like ciphers than speaking subjects, more like the two "noughts" to be discussed later.

7. Any account of the neo-avantgarde in America must consider the curious position of Philip Johnson, as both a contributor to the formalization of modernism and as a predecessor and sometimes sponsor to a younger generation of architects and critics that would dispute that reconstruction, most recently evident in his endorsement of the "deconstructivists." It is perhaps no accident that Johnson was strangely absent from any public or commercial role in the profession precisely during the period being discussed here. After the publication of an elaborate monograph on his collected works in 1966 Johnson seemed to disappear from the architectural scene for nearly a decade. His sudden reappearance is marked by his April Fool's Day postscript to *Five Architects* in 1974 and a lecture delivered at Columbia ("What Makes Me Tick") in 1975. The theme of the fetish, too, runs through Johnson's playful architecture. As early as 1963, in his commentary on the "false scale" pavilion he designed for his New Canaan estate, Johnson voices his distaste for the purely utilitarian ethic of "modern" design by discussing shoes: "Usefulness as a criterion condemns our art to a mere technological scheme to cover ourselves from the weather, much as to say that shoes should be practical, not hurtful and handsome. Actually, there exist shoes designed just for comfort and we all them for the hideously ugly monstrosities that they are . . . But I say, just as in footwear, we need beautiful, in addition to mildly useful, buildings. My pavilion I should wish to be compared to high-style, high-heeled evening slippers, preferably satin—a pleasure-giving object, designed for beauty and the enhancement of human, preferably blonde, beauty." Johnson, "Full Scale False Scale," *Writings* (New York: Oxford University Press, 1979), 251. Curiously, in the well-known photograph showing Johnson inside the four room pavilion that accompanied this article, Johnson appears to be standing in the room he identifies as "the Boudoir."

8. William Jordy, "Robert Venturi and the Decorated Shed," *The New Criterion* (May 1985): 58. For this "father," apparently, there can only be mothers—Denise Scott Brown has, for example, referred to Louis Kahn as Venturi's "architectural mother." See, "A Worm's Eye View of Recent Architectural History," *Architectural Record* (February 1984): 69–81.

9. Stanislaus von Moos, *Venturi, Rauch and Scott Brown: Buildings and Projects* (New York: Rizzoli International, 1987), 241. Vincent Scully has made a similar comparison in the introduction to Venturi's *Complexity and Contradiction in Architecture* (New York: Museum of Modern Art, 1966), which Scully describes as "probably the most important writing on the making of architecture since Le Corbusier's *Vers une Architecture*, of 1923." Scully, "The Shingle Style," 11.

10. Robert Venturi and Denise Scott Brown, *A View from the Campidoglio: Selected Essays, 1953–1984.* (New York: Harper and Row, 1984), 10. Scott Brown continues to say "[t]hat is why it needs reassessing on occasion." The following takes its invitation from her.

11. Vincent Scully, "The Failure of the Hero Architect," *Metropolitan Home* (November 1988): 200. Scully has projected his humanism onto a variety of projects, including one as improbable as Philip Johnson's Glass House. "[T]he Glass House is the heart of what Johnson believes in, which is nothing less than the ageless humanist dream stated in contemporary terms and embodied in contemporary form." Philip Johnson, *Writings* (New York: Oxford University Press, 1979), 8. For Scully, this humanist challenge involves "how to use technology in order to be free; how to shake off conceptual limitations in order to be released to all the choices of life and the magnificent rhythm of the natural world." (8)

12. This story has been recently retold in *The Architecture of Robert Venturi*, ed. by Christopher Mead (Albuquerque, NM: University of New Mexico Press, 1989), with essays by Scully, David Van Zanten, Neil Levine, Thomas Beeby, and Stephen Kieran.

13. The prospect of a talking car has recently become a reality. As described by Jean Baudrillard, the car moves from being an object of performance to an information network that "spontaneously" informs you of its general state and even of your general state, possibly refusing to function if you are not functioning well, the car as deliberating

consultant and partner in the general negotiation of a lifestyle, something—or someone: at this point there is no longer any difference—with which you are connected. The fundamental issue becomes the communication with the car itself, a perpetual test of the subject's presence with his own objects, an uninterrupted interface." Baudrillard, "The Ecstasy of Communication," *The Anti-Aesthetic*, ed. Hal Foster (Port Townsend, WA: Bay Press, 1983), 127.

14. Andreas Huyssen, "The Vamp and the Machine: Fritz Lang's *Metropolis*," *After the Great Divide* (Bloomington, IN: Indiana University Press, 1986), 71.

15. See Joseph Hudnut, "The Post–Modern House," *Architectural Record* (May 1945): 75.

16. The temporary frozen aspect of this still or snapshot is reiterated through its dominant orange–yellow palette, a restriction to the hues that would emerge first during the process of photographic development.

17. Though Hamilton's image (with the exception of the subject matter, self-conscious posing, and almost square format) seems to refer most explicitly to the home developing potential of the Polaroid Land Camera, the possibility for this kind of auto-documentation has been greatly expanded with the advent of home video. Recorded self-surveillance as testimony against oneself has appeared most recently, for example, in the legal problems of Rob Lowe and Robert Chambers, the "preppy murderer."

18. This agenda can be seen as still operative in the work of someone like Neil Levine, whose recovery of Frank Lloyd Wright is intended to open the canon of the International Style. See his "Abstraction and Representation in Modern Architecture: The International Style and Frank Lloyd Wright," *AA Files* 11 (January 1986): 3–21. Levine, who was a student of Scully's, proposes a humanist/romantic redefinition of modernism which is opposed to the recent recuperation of the Russian constructivists. For his part, Scully has characterized the "rickety little Deconstructivist show" as one aspect of the "recurrent manic-heroic twitches of the moribund International Style." Scully, "The Failure of the Hero Architect," *Metropolitan Home* (November 1988): 200.

19. Although there is not sufficient time to elaborate this here, the same need arises—namely, to be simultaneously outside and inside, transcendent and immanent, above and below—in other architectural techniques of this time, most notably the axonometric and topological systems that Eisenman employs. This oscillation is not surprising, of course, given the dual role of the architect-critic, who must both produce and reflect. As will be shown later, this new professional situation is registered in the attention given to the formal problem of the wall.

20. This structure appears consistently throughout Venturi's work. Describing his firm's addition to Cass Gilbert's Allen Art Museum at Oberlin Venturi writes: ". . . adding a wing to the art museum is like drawing a mustache on a Madonna. . . . [A] wing on a symmetrical Renaissance villa, like a bowler hat on a Venus, will never look correct." Here, the Madonna/Venus axis allows Venturi to invoke tactics used by the historical avant-garde in supplementing the woman's body (i.e., Duchamp's mustache and Magritte's bowler hat). See, "Plain and Fancy Architecture by Cass Gilbert and the Additions to the Allen Memorial Art Museum by Venturi and Rauch, at Oberlin," in *A View from the Campidoglio*, 51.

21. Venturi has repeatedly gendered the sign as female. "The Kolbe in the Barcelona Pavilion was a foil to the directed spaces. The message was mainly architectural. The diminutive signs in most Modern buildings contained only the most necessary messages, like LADIES, minor accents begrudgingly applied." Venturi, et al., *Learning from Las Vegas* (Cambridge, MA: MIT Press, 1972, rev. ed. 1977), 7. Venturi inverts this modern hierarchy by enlarging both the sign and the significance of the woman's body, both are rendered equivalent and supplant "Space as God" (the Father).

22. Robert Venturi, "A Buildingboard Involving Movies, Relics, and Space," *Architectural Forum* (April 1968): 77.

23. Venturi, *Complexity and Contradiction in Architecture* (New York: Museum of Modern Art, 1966), 88–89.

24. Additionally, the collapsed, superimposition of walls implies that Venturi is constructing as architecture of sequential events, and that, for example, the triple layering of the Guild House and Vanna Venturi residence correspond to three still "moments." Unlike the free movement through an abstract and uninterrupted space provided by a modernist like Mies, this represents movement through slices of time. A predecessor to the more fully cinematic and indexical structures of Eisenman, Venturi's work is the architectural equivalent to the early photographic studies of Edward Muybridge. In this, Venturi generates a kind of "spatialization of time," which Panofsky has identified as one of the defining characteristics of the cinema.

25. Tafuri, "'European Graffiti.' Five x Five = Twenty-five," *Oppositions* 5 (Summer 1976), 45.

26. Richard A Scheweder, "In Paris—Miniskirts of the Mind," *New York Times Book Review*, 8 January 1989.

27. William S. Burroughs, *Naked Lunch* (New York: Grove Press, 1959), 61. Benway reappears in 1987's *The Western Lands* as a member of the "Zoo Team," an animal transplant unit concerned with hybridization and mutation that includes a magician among its non-medical staff.

28. This gesture can be seen in the architectural practice of someone like John Hejduk who bisects the domestic residence, part unnecessary surgery and part interrupted trick, as in his One-Half House from 1966.

29. These opposed attitudes of magician-surgeon have recently become visible in the urban environment, again in relation to the wall, in the diverse practices of Richard Hass and Krzystof Wodiczko. Hass's painted murals, totalistic and illusory, are permanent celebrations of place. Loosely based on local formal vocabularies that nonetheless require places names to invoke identity, Hass's murals act as affirmative touristic emblems, and often participate in a beautification plan that accompanies financial reinvestment and gentrification. They are objects of contemplation. Wodiczko's mechanically projected fragments, on the other hand, are transitory interventions on

the urban environment that combine critical comment with humor. Appearing in the temporary and theatrical settling of night, Wodiczko's public projections usually engender discussion and debate among the spectators and passersby. They are sometimes unapproved (as the projection of the swastika on the pediment of the South African embassy), and frequently address the issues of homelessness and urban displacement. In this way, the projected parts of human anatomy "magically" enliven building facades with a critical (surgical) end in mind—quite opposite to Hass's trompe-l'oeil murals or Scully's ventriloquist act with Venturi's Trubeck and Wislocki Houses.

30. In general, this form of "rigorous" criticism tends only to reinstitute the aura and celebrate already canonic figures.

31. This procedure is not unrelated to Dali's paranoid-critical method that Rem Koolhaas rediscovers in *Delirious New York*. Equally, this generation of fictions has appeared in Peter Eisenman's current interest in "misreading," in the creation of "an architecture that is far more *real* than architecture ever is." Eisenman. "*Misreading* Peter Eisenman," *Houses of Cards* (New York: Oxford University Press, 1987), 186. Eisenman's hyperreal architecture is more real because it is surrounded by more misreadings, more reproductions. It is in an orbital state above and beyond reality in the same way that cinema or photorealism seem "more real than the real." Again, this emphasizes the need for Eisenman's work for documentation, the criterion of reproducibility, in order for it to exist at all. This provides the opportunity for a 'pata-architecture', an architecture of imaginary solutions (programmatic, contextual, functional, symbolic, typological, etc.), that can only be approached through a new articulation between criticism and object, a mutation in which neither one explains or has priority over the other: i.e., a practice in which neither exists.

32. This, too, may have been ironically predicted by Eisenman's insistence on the graphic erasure, or ghostly outlining, of the first of the doubled Ps in *Oppositions*, suggesting (among other things) zero positions. This is not surprising since an obsession with splitting and doubling has characterized a large proportion of neo-avantgarde practices and images, and represents a confession of their new dual role (as producer-critics) as well as a reflection on their historical moment as the second coming, or mirror stage, of the avant-garde. What should not be overlooked in this chance economy of doubling and splitting, however, is the implicit rhetoric of gambling or gaming (as opposed to work or production). After House X, Eisenman doubles down and draws two elevens—XIa and El Even Odd. As with the two noughts on the roulette wheel, the green that denies (constructivist?) red and black, Eisenman's even/odd hybrid ensures that all bets are covered and that there is no possibility of chance. This is a description of the world that it simultaneously inhabits; it takes advantage of the condition it names. Similarly, this rhetoric of gambling or chance permeates the work of Tafuri who invariably recognizes dual oppositions throughout history only to reduce them finally to a condition of identity. This also explains why so many of his sentences and paragraphs begin with some form of the following: "It is not just by chance that . . . ," "It is hardly by chance that . . . ," "It is not only by coincidence that. . . ,"etc. Chance and opposition are nullified by the double zero. In this way, perhaps, the fetish serves only to hide the lack of a lack. Thus, the problem with addressing the issue in the format "architecture and the fetish" (or "architecture and ideology," which amounts to the same thing since both derive from early modern master narratives) is that it assumes that something (else) is being covered or masked, that there is a truthful final and original condition. The question itself misleads in that it becomes the sign of a depth or difference that no longer operates, to the extent that it invites an interpretation that demands transformation or cure. But everything is already fixed, in all its senses.

Illustrations

1. Madelon Vriesendorp, *Flagrant delit*, from *Delirious New York*, 1978. Courtesy Rem Koolhaas.
2. Rene Magritte, *La Philosophie dans le boudoir*, 1947.
3. Robert Venturi, Trubek and Wislocki Houses, 1971–1972. All Venturi photographs courtesy Venturi, Scott Brown and Associates, Inc. unless otherwise noted.
4. Robert Venturi, Vanna Venturi House, 1962–1964 (Photo: Rollin R. La France, c. 1966).
5. Le Corbusier, Villa Stein, 1927.
6. Hubert Van Eyck, *Annunciation*, c. 1426. Courtesy National Gallery of Art, Washington.
7. *My Mother the Car*, NBC, 1965–1966. Globe Photo Agency, New York.
8. Raoul Hausmann, *Tatlin at Home*, 1920.
9. Hannah Hoch, *Pretty Maiden*, 1920.
10. Richard Hamilton, *Just What Is it That Makes Today's Homes So Different, So Appealing?*, 1956.
11. LLV Workshop, Tanya Billboard, c. 1968.
12. Robert Venturi, Lieb House, 1967 (front entrance).
13. Robert Venturi, Lieb House, 1967 (upstairs living area).
14. Robert Venturi, National Football Hall of Fame Entry, 1967 (front entrance elevation).
15. Robert Venturi, National Football Hall of Fame Entry, 1967 (interior arcade perspective).
16. Robert Venturi, Guild House, 1961–1965.
17. Robert Venturi, Fire Station #4, 1966–1967.
18. Richard Estes, *Double Self-Portrait*, 1976. Collection, The Museum of Modern Art, New York. Mr. and Mrs. Stuart M. Speiser Fund. Reprinted with permission.
19. Richard Estes, *Bus Reflections*, 1972. Courtesy Allen Stone Gallery, New York.
20. Peter Greenaway, *A Zed and Two Noughts*, 1985 (Oswald, Alba, and Oliver).

JENNIFER BLOOMER

Big Jugs[1]

I have given this paper two parts, which we might call theoretical and practical (a construction), for the benefit of those who think that architects are incapable of thinking about what they do and even less capable of talking about it; and for those who believe that nobody needs to talk about architecture, one should just DO it. If you fall into one of these categories, you may choose to read only the appropriate part. Good luck in deciding which one is which.

PART ONE

Western architecture is, by its very nature, a phallocentric discourse: containing, ordering, and representing through firmness, commodity, and beauty[2]; consisting of orders, entablature, and architrave; base, shaft, and capital; nave, choir, and apse; father, son, and spirit, world without end. Amen.

In the Garden of Eden there was no architecture. The necessity for architecture arose with the ordination of sin and shame, with dirty bodies. The fig leaf was a natural first impulse toward architecture, accustomed as it was to shading its vulvate fruit, its trunk and roots a complex woven construction of undulating forms. Was It the fig tree that was hacked up to build the primitive hut (that precursor of classical architecture)?

The primitive hut and all its begettings constitute a house of many mansions, a firm, commodious, and beautiful erection. The primitive hut is the house of my fathers. But there is the beginning of an intrusive presence in this house:

> *She transforms, she acts: the old culture will soon be the new. She is mixed up in dirty things; she has no cleanliness phobia—the proper housecleaning attacks that hysterics sometimes suffer. She handles filth, manipulates wastes, buries placentas, and burns the cauls of new born babies for luck. She makes partial objects useful, puts them back in circulation—properly. En voila du propre! What a fine mess![3]*

Julia Kristeva has written:

> *As capitalist society is being economically and politically choked to death, discourse is wearing thin and heading for collapse at a more rapid rate than ever before. Philosophical finds, various modes of 'teaching,' scientific or*

aesthetic formalisms follow one upon another, compete, and disappear without leaving either a convinced audience or noteworthy disciples. Didacticism, rhetoric, dogmatism of any kind, in any 'field' whatsoever, no longer command attention. They have survived, and perhaps will continue to survive, in modified form, throughout Academia. Only one language grows more and more contemporary: the equivalent, beyond a span of thirty years, of the language of Finnegans Wake.[4]

Broadcast throughout the text of Finnegans Wake are thousands of seedy little t's, those bits of letter written, devoured, excreted, and pecked by the hen. They are little micturition sounds, tiny trabeation signs. To make those posts on beams properly classical, let us add the prescribed third part: the T becomes an I. The I, the ego, the I beam, the gaze, the image fixer, the instrument of fetish. When I was a child in church, I was told that the great golden "I" embroidered on the altar cloth stood for "INRI." I wondered why the church didn't spell its Henry with an H. Hen ri—the hen laughs. Ha ha ha ha—the sound of H is pure expiration: laughter, sighing, and the way we breathe when we are giving birth to our children. BODY LANGUAGE. The sound of H is more than mere pronunciation of three marks on a page—two parallels, one bridge. It is a mark itself of invisible flows.

Much as David Byrne perhaps "eggoarchicistically" burns down the house, James Joyce has enjoisted an other construction:

> *The boxes, if I may break the subject gently, are worth about fourpence pourbox but I am inventing a more patent process, foolproof and pryperfect (I should like to ask that Shedlock Homes person who is out for removing the roofs of our criminal classics by what deductio ad domunum he hopes de tacto to detect anything unless he happens of himself, movibile tectu, to have a slade off) after which they can be reduced to a fragment of their true crust by even the youngest of Margees if she will take plase to be seated and smile if I please.*[5]

Here is the hatchery. Let Us Deconstruct: Margee is the marginal one, taking her place, seated and smiling, faking, being woman as constituted by the symbolic order. *Movibile tectu*: homophonous to *horribile dictu* (horrible to tell, unspeakable). This is a passage from Virgil repeated throughout the *Aeneid* much as the hen's letter is scattered throughout the text of *Finnegans Wake*. And *movibile tectu* is also moving touch: the moving finger writes, and, having writ, moves on. Architectural references abound: boxes, Shed, Lock (as in locked out of the house), Homes, roofs, classics, domunum, slade.

The hatchery is an apparatus of overlay of architecture, writing, and the body. The hatchery is a kind of architectural anti-type, i.e., it refers to a kind of built structure (the chicken house), but the structure to which it refers does not belong to the domain of the architect. It is a house, but not architecture, and its

Jennifer Bloomer

relationship to the primitive hut is mediated to the point of extreme tentativeness, primarily because the form of the hatchery is irrelevant. The hatchery is not bound or bounded by theory, but is a para-theoretical device. The hatchery is that which is not represented when the architecture-making is done. The hatchery is Work in Progress, a critical instrument, intrusive and elucidating. It refers to the place of the hatching of chickens from eggs, the place of the life flow, a dirty (soiled) cacophonous place full of litter, the residue of life (eggshells, excrement, cast-off feathers, uneaten food). In this sense, it is a kind of alchemical vessel, a container of ingredients for the Philosopher's Stone (*un vaisseau de pierre*). Its floor is inscribed with the imprints of chicken feet (hatchings and cross-hatchings).

The hatchery is a writing machine. The biddies, the chicks, scratch marks in the dirt. These hieroglyphs constitute an historical document, a mapping and a marking of movement. This act of hatching resembles and belongs to the acts of etching, drawing, and writing. It is the act of the hatching of lines and the hatching of plots.

The body is, in a sense, a multiply-constituted hatchery, a messy assemblage of flows—blood, organic matter, libidinal, synaptic, psychic. The metaphor for the throat—the primary entrance portal—is the hatch, as in "down the hatch." This hatch is a door or passage. We describe our bodies and our constructions in terms of each other, with words as passages between one and the other. Writes of passage, hatcheries all.

Alice Jardine:

> [W]hat fiction has always done—the incorporation and rejection of that space [the space of schizophrenia, the libidinal economy, that which has begun to threaten authorship, that which is connoted as feminine—see Jardine, p. 88] as grounds for figurability—new theoretical discourses, with rapidly increasing frequency, have also been doing. Seeing themselves as no longer isolated in a system of loans and debts to former master truths, these new discourses in formation have foregrounded a physis, a space no longer passive but both active and passive, undulating, folded over upon itself, permeable: the self-contained space of eroticism.[6]

The hatchery is a bridge between the sacred and the voluptuous, between *physis* and *techne*.

In Frank Baum's *The Wizard of Oz*, Dorothy's house becomes disconnected at the point of the hatch (trap-door to the cellar underneath) and floats and rises gently in the center of the cyclone. When the house falls, it kills the wicked witch and Dorothy is construed as a sorceress in a country that is not civilized, and therefore retains a population of sorceresses, witches, and wizards.

Dorothy falls and Alice falls, but into other worlds—worlds of magic and strangeness. Adam, Lucifer, Humpty Dumpty, and Icarus fell to less desirable ends.

The boys attempt to rise to power and fail, lose, fall from grace. The girls drop out, fall down the hatch, use the exits, find the dreamworld of condensation and displacement, of strangeness, of *délire*.[7] The position to take is perched at the rim of the hole, at the moment of the closing of the trap door, ready to fall, not to fall from, but INTO. The "fall from" is hierarchical and you can hurt yourself. The "fall into" is labyrinthine, dreamy, a dancing fall, a delirious fall.

"Her rising: is not erection. But diffusion. Not the shaft. The Vessel."[8] The Hatchery is both vessel and erection (the topology of erection is vesicular flow, after all), but it is neither of these things in the formal sense. The form must remain undefined to escape co-optation. (The aestheticization of the political is a patriarchal sleight of hand power play against which Walter Benjamin warned us long ago.) We can, however, emblematize it with its initial letter. The H is an I in which the shaft has been allowed to rest horizontal for a moment, forming a vessel, a container, a bridge, a conduit.

The Hatchery might be, but cannot be, classified into categories. Political, unauthorized, and unauthored, it is about acts, not images; transitory, it is movement, but is not a movement. Hacking at the edges of the architecture/state apparatus, it is all these categories. It is political and collective and moving.

Barnacles, engulfings, underminings, intrusions: Minor Architecture.[9] Collective, anonymous, authorless, scratched on the city and the landscape, they are hatched not birthed. (They are illegitimate—without father.) Bastard Constructions. In matriarchal societies, there is no concept of legitimacy. One is legitimate by virtue of existence. No-one knows a single father; all males are the nurturing fathers of all children. Children are born of the mother; they are legitimate by virtue of having made the passage from inside to out.

"Wee peeps"[10] appear locally upon the landscape of The Gaze. Wee peeps: we peeks, small chickens (chicks), brief glances, a hint of impropriety—micturition in public. Tattoos upon the symbolic order. They are the "lens" that "we need the loan of . . . to see as much as the hen saw."[11] Like minor literature, or the little girls on Tintorelli's stair in *The Trial,* or the twenty-eight little girl shadows of Isabelle, or the rainbow girls in *Finnegans Wake.* Tattoos. T-t-t's.

"This battering babel allower the door and sideposts":[12] the hatchery, the place of babes and babble, both allows and lowers the supporting structure of the entrance to the House.

A biddy architecture (a surd and absurd[13] architecture): Around midnight, Atlanta, Georgia. Moving along Techwood Drive, the access road running parallel to Interstate 75–85, and accessing the House of Ted Turner. On the right: plantation image, tasteful, white sign with Chippendale frame—"The Turner Broadcasting System." On the left: parallax view of trees silhouetted against the

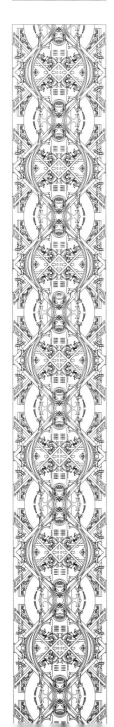

glow of the here submerged interstate highway and, beyond, the city lights. Glimpsed among the trees: small constructions of sticks and draped membranes through which the lights osmose—so strange that you might be hallucinating. Against the membranes, blocking the glow with jarringly recognizable blackness: human figures here and there, existing for the moment between the lines.

ART TWO

In Florida, as perhaps in other places, we are situated upon a most peculiar landscape. We stand upon a ground not of rock resting upon rock, but of the merest slice of solidity barely breaking the surface of the surrounding sea. Furthermore, the ground beneath our feet is not reliable, not the solid architecture of stone piled upon stone, carrying its loading in the proper compressive fashion, that we like our ground to be. It is in fact an architecture of holes and crypts, filling and emptying with fluids, an architecture delineated by suction and secretion, of solids, fluids, and gases, in such a complex and everchanging configuration that to pin it down with a word seems illogical. But it is named by a word: Alachua,[14] a word the previous residents of this place chose. Alachua: a vessel or jug. Alachua, a land of filling and emptying, of holes and crypts, a place where the superimposition of "order" is ridiculous. A place where entire buildings are swallowed up, disappear into the surface of the ground, leaving behind only pock marks, that will eventually fill with fluid. The consideration of such an architecture is not about imbuing a mundane thing with pumped-up significance, nor about projecting an image of the place. It is about how it works. Not about what it means or what it looks like, but what it does. The following construction is a mapping of this territory. It is the landscape of Edgar Poe, a territory of significant voids.[15]

This construction consists of a collision of three texts: an essay by Martin Heidegger titled "The Thing"; a character from Angela Carter's *Nights at the Circus*, Fanny Four-Eyes, who sports eyes on her breasts where nipples properly should be; and a third, the text of architecture, which in its over-Booked and boxed-in state, is pocked with more booby traps than those of us who practice it would like to think. It is possible that there is a fourth text, an oscillating text, quite "rudely forc'd."[16]

In a happenstance that gives me more pleasure than I can say, this text intersects with the conclusion of Catherine Ingraham's review, called "Milking Deconstruction, or Cow Was the Show?,"[17] of the 1988 Deconstructivism Show at the Museum of Modern Art. Here, Ingraham constructs a situation in which the contemporary architectural phenomenon of "Deconstructivism" is allegorized in the contemporary corporate agricultural phenomenon of the "necessity" to re-

engineer the structure of the new hormone-injected, super milk-giving cows in order to support their mammoth udders.

> *The idea of the cow as a thing—like the cow-thing [a jug] we fill with milk and set on our dinner table—is what makes the crude tampering with its bone structure possible . . . Equally, the idea of deconstruction as a thing that can be built results in the crude surgeries of deconstructivism. It will ultimately be the shift in the idea of architectural structure—its dematerialization—that will interfere most substantially with the material surfaces of architecture, not so many jugs and pitchers cast in the shape of something called deconstructivism.*[18]

Jugs and things are the objects of Heidegger's essay. If you will allow, I will recast this large and intricate vessel into a state that will accommodate an apprehension of a certain subtext. Despite the closure of space and time in the modern world, there is no nearness. We perceive that things are near to us, "[b]ut what is a thing?"[19] "A jug is a thing. What is the jug? We say: a vessel, something of the kind that holds something else within it."[20] "As a vessel the jug stands on its own as self-supporting."[21] When we put it into our field of perception either through immediacy or representation, it becomes an object, yet it remains a vessel. The jug as a thing holds something. It is a container that must be made. When we understand it as a constructed vessel, we apprehend it as a thing, not as an object. We can never learn how the jug is by looking at its outward appearance; "[t]he vessel's thingness does not lie at all in the material of which it consists, but in the void that holds."[22] "Only a vessel . . . can empty itself."[23] "How does the jug's void hold? It holds by taking what is poured in. It holds by keeping and retaining what it took in. The void holds in a twofold manner: taking and keeping. The word 'hold' is therefore ambiguous."[24] "To pour from the jug is to give."[25] "But the gift of the outpouring is what makes a jug a jug.[26] Even the empty jug suggests the gift by a "nonadmission" of which "a scythe . . . or a hammer is incapable."[27] The thing is "nestling, malleable, pliant, compliant . . ."[28] The thing is "modestly compliant."[29] "Inconspicuously compliant is the thing."[30] "Nestling" is the thing.

The logo of the Nestle Corporation—known for its milk-like products—depicts a perfectly round nest—a domestic vessel—resting on a branch from which three leaves grow in trinitary symmetry. Nestled in the nest are two small birds with straining bodies and eager beaks. Perched on the rim is a large mother bird in the position of offering something to her young. But, look closely at this picture: the mother holds nothing in her beak. The logo is a hieroglyph that gives up a secret. The logo is a figuration of the corporation's activities in third world countries, where a small supply of infant formula, which carries with it the image of first world magic, is given "free" to women who have just given birth. Inconspicuously—not readily noticeable, especially by "eyes which do not see"[31]—the Nestle Corporation

makes empty vessels. The dry, petrified udder sells more man-made milk. This gift, mixed with promise and tainted water, is an outpouring of forced consumption, sickness, and death. The women are perhaps comforted by the "gift" of breasts imbued with first-world aura: breasts which have not been sucked are privileged as objects. They are firm and erect; they stick out.

*T*WO WAYS OF LOOKING AT A JUG:

Aesthetic: *"Stick 'em out just a little more. Yeah, now pull your tummy in all the way and let it out just a tad."* Lifted and separated from the wall, the things appear twice their actual size and full and round as if to bursting. *"Yeah. Now really push 'em up, hold your breath, keep your chin down and give me the look. Give it to me, baby, give it to me, yeah, yeah. Terrific!"* Click!

Scientific: *"Now, you've got to get the whole thing up on the plate. It'll feel a little cold, but it'll be over in a minute."* The glass plate descends, pressing down, pressing, pressing the thing out to a horrifying, unrecognizable state: thin and flat, a broad, hideous slice of solidity criss-crossed with shocking blue lines. *"Yes, that's it. Now hold your breath. Good!"* Click!

"'Well now that's done: and I'm glad it's over.'" [32]

What is the secret that the firm, erect, sticking out thing holds? Unused, it is a frontier, where no man has gone before. What is the secret that lies beneath the power of this image, this object? What most desired and most feared thing is masked behind the desire to be the first, or the biggest? What does (M)other lack?

What is the secret that "oozes from the box?" Deleuze and Guattari:

The secret must sneak, insert, or introduce itself into the arena of public forms; it must pressure them and prod known subjects into action . . . [S]omething must ooze from the box, something will be perceived through the box or in the half-opened box. [33]

Corporate architecture is a certain return of the repressed.

In Thomas Pynchon's novel *V.*, a novel whose entire four hundred and sixty-three pages are devoted to a search for a figure which seems to be a woman, perhaps the mother of the protagonist, who exists only in traces and hints. V herself is masked by a seemingly infinite constellation of guises, forming the fetish construction that is the novel itself. Through the text there walks a figure known as the Bad Priest. Walks until, at a certain point of intersection, he falls down and falls apart, revealing himself to be a beautiful young woman who is in turn revealed, by the children and the imagination of the narrator who dismantle her body, as a machinic assemblage of objects: glittering stones and precious metals, clocks, balloons, and lovely silks. The Bad Priest is a fetish construction mirroring the

novel. As Alice Jardine has pointed out, it is "an assemblage of the dead objects that have helped hold together the narrative thus far."[34] The Bad Priest and V are reconstituted objects of desire, constructions of what is most desired and most feared. They are a rewriting of the urge to the aesthetic. (You will recall that Aesthetics begins with the assemblage of the most beautiful, most perfect [and malleable, modestly compliant] woman by cutting the most desirable parts off many women and gathering them to make one woman-thing.) Like Pandora, whose box was not a box, but a jar, or jug. When the Bad Priest falls, the children cry, "It's a lady," and then: "She comes apart."[35] Into "[a] heap of broken images."[36]

"It's a Lady." Consider the Statue of Liberty, a fetish construction: she is a thing placed on a pedestal—to "lift and separate," to put on display. She is a spectacle. She is the hyper-reification of Luce Irigaray's gold-plated (in this case, copper-clad) woman: woman's body covered with commodities (make-up, fashion, capital, gold).

> The cosmetics, the disguises of all kinds that women cover themselves with are intended to deceive, to promise more value than can be delivered. . . . Her body transformed into gold to satisfy his autoerotic, scopophiliac, and possessive instincts.[37]

This image of "Liberty for All" contains a secret, a purloined letter ingeniously hidden because it is there, in plain sight, a secret that calls into question the concepts of "Liberty" and "All." Beneath the surface of this woman's skin, beneath the implants which pump up the image, lies a "creeping disaster," [Irigaray] a crabby invasion, a crabgrass, a rhizome.

The Statue of Liberty is an allegory of desire and fear. It is a container, "a place where something is about to happen."[38] It is structure and envelope, image and machine. A gift. A Lady. And she comes apart.

1.

Jennifer Bloomer

N THE SUMMER OF 1987, a consortium of French institutions (including L'Institut Francais d'Architecture) co-sponsored an international competition for the design of cultural artifacts commemorating the bicentenary of the French Revolution. The multidisciplinary and international intentions behind the competition were reinforced by the diversity of the jury, which ranged from the philosopher Jean Baudrillard to the structural engineer Peter Rice, and included writers, musicians, visual artists, and business people. The instructions for the production of the commemorative artifacts were vague, leaving site, event commemorated, media, and dimensions at the discretion of the authors. Attracted by the indeterminacy, two friends—Durham Crout, a former student presently teaching architecture at Clemson University and pursuing a Ph.D. at the University of Pennsylvania, and Robert Segrest—and I decided to participate.

Our project began as a project of exchange. As citizens of the United States constructing a monument to the French Revolution, we began with the simple idea of returning the gesture of the gift given by the French to commemorate the American Revolution. This gift, the Statue of Liberty, immediately generated a series of correspondences to other concepts delineated by the idea of gift: woman as presentation (both in the sense of the allegorical figure of Liberty and in the sense of woman as spectacle, as object of the gaze), woman as currency (both in the sense of the medium of exchange and in the sense of a flow that must be controlled, woman as fetish construction to be bestowed upon the imagination. We were struck by the way in which several constructs of power coincided in this woman-thing: war, aesthetics, the monumental, the reification of the female, history, the symbolic. We chose to commemorate an event of the French Revolution that bore potential correspondences to this construction of constructs, an event described by Marilyn French in *Beyond Power:*[38]

> When, on October 5 [1789], the market women discovered there was no bread
> in Paris, six thousand of them marched the twelve miles to Versailles to protest
> to the king personally. He promised to help them, and they marched trium-
> phantly back to Paris with the royal family in tow.[39]

The itinerary that led to this choice is germane to an understanding of the project. Continuing along our line of the gift as generator, we selected nine sites on the body of woman/Liberty that are conventionally construed as (partial) objects of desire: eyes, lips, breasts, vulva, etc. These nine sites were made to correspond to nine sites of revolutionary points of intensity around the city of Paris through an operation involving sight lines, focal points, and the lens (a glassy instrument and the "mechanical" apparatus of the objectifying gaze). We then made nine incisions upon the body of the Statue of Liberty, slicing through each of the nine sites to produce a generating section. The irony of the similarity of our operation

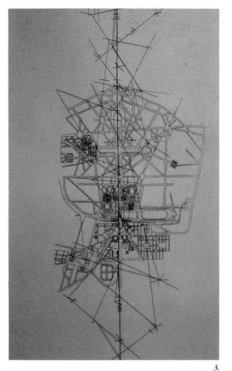

2.   3.

to those of slasher films and pornography was not lost upon us. The commentary of our work upon the recent work of contemporary architects whose work is tethered to the "aura" of mutilated and murdered women, we hope is not lost upon you. The nine sections were then to produce nine objects, to form a constellation of partial objects which, in their assemblage, would form a certain "gift" to the French. As is the way with well-laid plans, for a host of reasons including both fatigue and the powerful correspondence of the section through the eye and the site at the Palace at Versailles upon which it fell, we diverged from our original intentions and chose to operate only upon the eye and the march of the six thousand market women upon Versailles. The eye of the woman bears with it, after all, the potential to return the gaze; to return not merely in a sense of the conventional female acquiescence in sexual discourse, but also to re-turn, to deflect the power of the male gaze through a re-turn of the repressed, through the ex-orbitance of the female gaze. There is then in the project something of a reversal of the mechanics of the fascinus, a phallus-shaped amulet for warding off the "evil eye" of the fascinating woman. The evil eye, and to whom it belongs, is called into question.

It is the *unseen* in the body that is critical here. The sectioning of the statue is an act of incision and release. The incision marks the temporal and geographical point at which the image of the body gives way to the possibilities of the body. It becomes a gift of another kind, an insidious gift, with unseen agents hiding within, like the Trojan Horse. This hollow vessel, this monument, this

Jennifer Bloomer

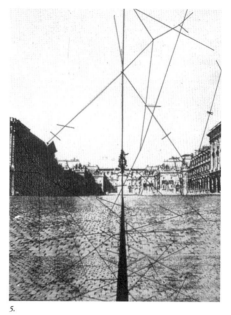

4.

5.

gift to the state, holds within it the potential of undermining the state. In the Trojan Horse, the body masks the body politic. The Trojan Horse is a viral architecture: a sleek protein coat with invasive content.

The incision marking the initiation of generation is repeated as an incising inscription. A slash three hundred meters long and a meter square in section is made on the Palace grounds. This repetition is simultaneously a reflection (an other kind of repetition) of an already-there gash in the earth: the Grand Canal, a commanding axis of inscription terminating in a statue. Thus, that which marks the termination of the grand axis is the same (vessel, statue) as that which marks the initiation of our project. And again, this identity is marked in reverse, setting the project into interminable reflexivity: the western end of the trench stops abruptly at the base of an other statue: that of Louis Quatorze atop a, perhaps now suspicious, horse. The new incision is a reflection of the old; the radical project is a mimicry of the State project. Furthermore, it is a rational response to the existing topography: our trench is a physically inscribed reflection of that which is marked by the relationship of the incision of the Grand Canal and the vertical slicing plane of the west (mirrored) wall of the Hall of Mirrors. In other words, we have taken the image of what one would see if one could see through the mirror and projected it back into the world before the mirror, reversing the customary relationship of "reality" and "image" in the mirror. In this geography of the imagination, the idea that the mirror is utterly contained within its grandiose vessel—the Palace—is simultaneously negligible and crucial.

The reflection works at another level as well. If one renders malleable the word for our gift, *un cadeau*, into a Franco-Italian hybrid of *ca d'eau*, there is here a house of water (a body), which parodies the wateriness, the flow, of the Grand Canal.

82

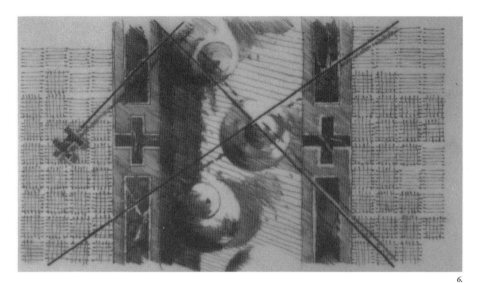

6.

7.

A *ca d'eau* is a house of currency. The trench functions as a monumental pissoir, open to the public in a public place. But being pissed off, here, is a redundant gesture. Nestled (modestly and compliantly) in the floor of the trench are six thousand vessels, with pear-like shapes and copper skins. Each is lined with mirror tain and glass and each is full to bursting with body fluids. Their bodily secrets allow them to laugh away or write off the oppression of being pissed on. These reproducing cells (vessels, fluid-filled uteri) mirror a something disastrous going on beneath the surface of the court of history, of power. It is the injection into a Revolution of "Feed Our Children." An injection of what is more "powerful than" (beyond) power. A giving suck, an other, although not the other, side of a suck taken. A gift.

Jennifer Bloomer

8.

9.

Its borders incised with alchemical glyphs signifying moons and months and body fluids, and marked by criss-crossing sutures of iron rods, this slice of void barely breaking the surface tension of the surrounding sea gives up its secret, a secret marked, as things which must remain properly hidden often are, with an X. The X is an emblem of Heidegger's fourfold, in which "each of the four mirrors in its own way the presence of the others."[40] X is a generic substitute for a thing. The thing is "nestling, malleable, pliant, compliant, nimble." Heidegger suggests circularity (O), but there is an X hidden here, an unknown, a secret. Heidegger's thing folds the fourfold along a hinge, which he suggests is a mirroring. An X hinged is two Vs folded at the point of intersection, the place where the secret is both enfolded and released. X is the doubled perspective on two canals intersecting in a mirror. It is a vanishing point. To X is "to delete, cancel, or obliterate with a series of x's."[41] X marks the (blind) spot(s) of history. "Cross your heart"—and hope to die and stick your finger in your eye. X is a cartoon convention marking "lidless eyes"[42] blinded by a surprise or blow to the head. As Catherine Ingraham has pointed out, the criss-cross of heavy mascara marks "eyes which do not see"—eyes which do not look beyond the look. X is a mark of non-identity, a non-identifying signature, like that of a person who is identified by the name of her father which, in a mirroring, is replaced by the name of her husband. Yet X is a chiasmus, signifying the alchemical androgyne—"blind, throbbing between two lives . . ."[43] X is the mark of Xantippe, who dumped a pot of piss on the head of her husband, Socrates. X is a kiss, both a "patronising"[44] and a nurturing gesture. A puckering, a sucking, an undulating architecture of solids, liquids, and gases.

84

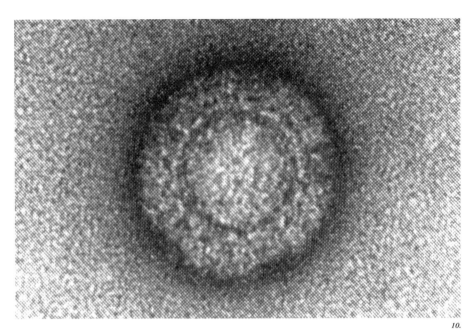

10.

A reverse *fascinus*, warding off the evil eye represented by the eye of the "one-eyed trouser snake" of Joyce, the Cyclopean eye of power invested in the Palace—the project is a defetishizing move, inviting the (male) body, refusing the power structure of the phallus that represses and corrupts the male body, and displaying the profound return of the repressed of the female body through an obscuring, a darkening, of the image, and a display of the generative—the jug is not a thing, but a magical machine—an interwoven system of apparatuses, a text.

'And Schreck would say: "Look at him, Fanny." So Fanny would take off her blindfold and give him a beaming smile.

'Then Madame Schreck would say: "I said, look at him, Fanny." At which she'd pull up her shift.

'For, where she should have had nipples, she had eyes.

'Then Madame Schreck would say: "Look at him properly, Fanny." Then those two other eyes of hers would open.

'They were a shepherd's blue, same as the eyes in her head; not big, but very bright.

'I asked her once, what did she see with those mammillary eyes, and she says: "Why, same as with the top ones but lower down.[45]

Jennifer Bloomer

Footnotes

1. This is the expanded (or augmented) text of a lecture called "Jugs" that I gave for the "Body/Space/Machine" Symposium held at the University of Florida in March 1989. The expanded version, called "Big Jugs," was delivered as a lecture at Princeton University in October 1989. A substantial portion of the implant comes from a paper, "Architecture, Writing, The Body," delivered in the session, "Forecasting the Direction of Architectural Theory," at the Annual Meeting of the Association of Collegiate Schools of Architecture in Miami 1987.

2. In the pages of an alumni newsletter from the University of Virginia's School of Architecture, there appeared recently a stinging critique of the current state of the grove of academe: that the students are engaged in producing "flaccid classicism." Webster's Third tells us that "flaccid" suggests a lack of firmness and stiffness or vigor and force. So, we might deduce that the architectural projects being produced at Virginia are, to the alumnus' eye, ones in which the first Vitruvian requisite is missing. An architecture, then, of *commoditas* and *venustas*, but no *firmitas*. But is there any other reading of this clearly pejorative phrase?

3. Hélène Cixous and Catherine Clément, *The Newly Born Woman*, trans. Betsy Wing, (Manchester: Manchester University Press, 1986 [1975]), 167. The translator points out that the phrase "*En voila du propre!*" (the English equivalent of which is "What a fine mess!") is used in the text in places where that which is considered "appropriate" is called into question.

4. Julia Kristeva, *Desire in Language: A Semiotic Approach to Art and Literature*, ed. Leon Roudiez, (New York: Columbia University Press, 1980), 92.

5. James Joyce, *Finnegan's Wake,* (New York: Viking Press, 1965 [1939]), 165.30–166.02.

6. Alice Jardine, *Gynesis: Configurations of Woman and Modernity* (Ithaca, NY: Cornell University Press, 1985), 100.

7. See Jean-Jacques Lecercle, *Philosophy Through the Looking Glass: Language, nonsense, desire* (London: Hutchinson and Co., 1985). Lecercle locates délire: "Délire, then, is at the frontier between two languages, the embodiment of the contradiction between them. Abstract language is systematic; it transcends the individual speaker, separated from any physical or material origin, it is an instrument of control, mastered by a regulating subject. Material language, on the other hand, is unsystematic, a series of noises, private to individual speakers, not meant to promote communication, and therefore self-contradictory, 'impossible' like all 'private languages.' . . . Language which has reverted to its origin in the human body, where the primary order reigns." (44–45)

8. Cixous and Clément, *The Newly Born Woman*, 88.

9. The term "minor architecture" is both properly deduced from architectural historians' conventional use of the term "major architecture" to refer to canonical buildings in the history of architecture, and is illegitimately appropriated from Gilles Deleuze's and Felix Guattari's concept of minor literature in, *Kafka: Toward a Minor Literature*, trans. Dana Polan, (Minneapolis: University of Minnesota Press, 1986 [1975]) .

    Minor literature is writing that takes on the conventions of a major language and subverts it from the inside. Deleuze's and Guattari's subject is the work of Franz Kafka, a Jew writing in German in Prague in the early part of this century. Minor literature possesses three dominant characteristics: l. It is that which a minority constructs within a major language, involving a deterritorialization of that language. Deleuze and Guattari compare Prague German to American Black English. 2. Minor literatures are intensely political: "[I]ts cramped space forces each individual intrigue to connect immediately to politics. The individual concern thus becomes all the more necessary, indispensable, magnified because a whole other story is vibrating within it." (17) 3. Minor literatures are collective assemblages; everything in them takes on a collective value.

    Deleuze and Guattari describe two paths of deterritorialization. One is to "artificially enrich [the language], to swell it up through all the resources of symbolism, of oneirism, of esoteric sense, of a hidden signifier." (19) This is a Joycean approach. The other is to take on the poverty of a language and take it further, "to the point of sobriety." (19) This is Kafka's approach. Deleuze and Guattari then reject the Joycean as a kind of closet reterritorialization which breaks from the people, and go all the way with Kafka.

    In transferring such a concept to architecture, already more simply material and with more complex relationships to "the people" and to pragmatics, I believe it necessary to hang onto both possibilities, shuttling between them. This may begin to delineate a line of scrimmage between making architectural objects and writing architectonic texts. What a minor architecture would be is a collection of practices that follow these conditions.

10. Joyce, 006.31–32.

11. Ibid., 112.01–2.

12. Ibid., 064.09.

13. That is, a voiceless, irrational construction characterized by a lack of agreement with accepted ideas (among other things). The relationships between the surd/absurd and architecture have been theorized by Jeffrey Kipnis. This represents the palest of allusions to his work.

14. My house is located a stone's throw from one of the numerous sinkholes in Alachua County, Florida. The architecture building at the University of Florida, where I work, is located at the edge of another. "Alachua" is a Seminole word meaning "jug."

15. See Edgar Allan Poe's *The Narrative of Arthur Gordon Pym*, for example.

16. T. S. Eliot, "The Waste Land," *The Waste Land and Other Poems*, (New York: Harcourt, Brace and World, 1962 [1922]), 37.

17. Catherine Ingraham, "Milking Deconstruction, or Cow Was the Show?," *Inland Architect* (September/October 1988).

18. Ibid., 65.

19. Martin Heidegger, "The Thing," *Poetry, Language, Thought*, trans. Albert Hofstadter, (New York: Harper and Row, 1971), 166.

20. Ibid.

21. Ibid., 167.

22. Ibid., 169.

23. Ibid.

24. Ibid., 171.

25. Ibid., 172.

26. Ibid.

27. Ibid.

28. Ibid., 180.

29. Ibid., 182.

30. Ibid.

31. This phrase refers to the well-known chapter from Le Corbusier's *Vers une architecture* and to Catherine Ingraham's critique of it in "The Burdens of Linearity," a paper presented at the Chicago Institute for Architecture and Urbanism (Skidmore, Owings and Merrill Foundation) Working Session on Contemporary Architectural Theory, September 1988, as well as to its more transparent referent, the eye of power which sees only that which it chooses to see.

32. Eliot, *The Wasteland*, 39.

33. Deleuze and Guattari, *A Thousand Plateaus* (*Capitalism and Schizophrenia*), trans. Brian Massumi, (Minneapolis: University of Minnesota Press, 1987 [1980]), 287.

34. Jardine, *Gynesis*, 251.

35. Thomas Pynchon, *V.* (1963; reprint, New York: Bantam Books, 1981), 320–321.

36. Eliot, *The Wasteland*, 30.

37. Luce Irigaray, *Speculum of the Other Woman*, trans. Gillian C. Gill, (Ithaca, NY: Cornell University Press, 1985), 114.

38. These are the words of Aldo Rossi, whose obsession with the idea of architecture as vessel is well-known and well-documented. See *A Scientific Autobiography*, trans. Lawrence Venuti, (Cambridge, MA: M.I.T. Press, 1981).

39. Marilyn French, *Beyond Power: On Women, Men, and Morals* (New York: Ballantine Books, 1985), 191.

40. Heidegger, *Poetry, Language, Thought,* 179.

41. From the *American Heritage Dictionary*.

42. Eliot, *The Wasteland*, 34.

43. Ibid., 38. The androgyne here is Tiresias, blinded because his androgynous experience led him to speak the unspeakable (that the female's pleasure—*jouissance*—is greater than that of the male). The complete phrase from Eliot is: "At the violet hour, when the eyes and back / Turn upward from the desk, when the human engine waits / Like a taxi throbbing waiting / I Tiresias, though blind, throbbing between two lives, / Old man with wrinkled female breasts, can see / At the violet hour, the evening hour that strives / Homeward, and brings the sailor home from sea."

44. Ibid., 39.

45. Angela Carter, *Nights at the Circus* (New York: Penguin Books, 1984), 69.

Illustrations

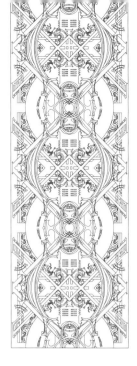

MARK WIGLEY

Theoretical Slippage: The Architecture Of The Fetish

ETISHIZING ARCHITECTURE

What is it to import the slippery word *fetish* into architectural discourse and enter the ongoing debate within critical theory? Do we have anything to offer in exchange? Which institutional secrets would be maintained by such a transaction? What improprieties would it cover?

For a start, it is unclear which sense of the word should be translated here: anthropological, philosophical, sociological, religious, psychiatric, aesthetic, economic or psychoanalytic? But perhaps even to ask such a question is already to resist the effects of a term coined at the intersection of discourses rather than within them. From its first use in the travelogues of European traders in Africa to its appearance in the recent interdisciplinary work in journals of critical theory, the word has always been produced in the face, or rather, facelessness, of the "other." It marks the inability of one discourse to fully incorporate another by transforming it into a definable object that can be placed within a field, the irreducible excess of that which is other precisely because it confounds such placement. Marking that which cannot be placed, its own "place" lies in the gaps between discourses, the fragile and therefore continuously renegotiated scenes of exchange, interstitial spaces that are themselves at once the first products, and the very possibility, of any economy. As William Pietz argues, "The fetish must be viewed as proper to no historical field other than that of the history of the word itself, and to no discrete society or culture, but to a cross-cultural situation formed by the ongoing encounter of the value codes of radically different social orders."[1]

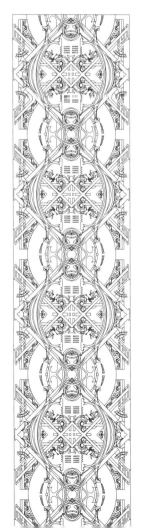

The term *fetish*, which emerged in the sixteenth century in the narrow strip along the West Coast of Africa acting as the site of exchange between Europe and Africa, was first used to describe apparently perverse practices of indigenous cultures in a way that allowed commerce to take place. Indeed, it continues to allow different cultural institutions to take place, to maintain their identity—the sense that they constitute a place—in the face of the radical threats that they pose to each other.

Such threats are necessarily spatial. The interstitial sites within which the word fetish operates do not lie simply between two spaces but between two kinds of space, two cultural systems for the production of space, and the word serves only one of those spatialities. While each economy appears to be based on exchange between cultures, each is invariably a scene of exploitation. The use of the word marks the ability of one spatial system to master another by redefining it, translating it into familiar terms in order to domesticate it. The term's first use, for example, paralleled the mapping of the "dark" "interior" of Africa. The territory was literally annexed by the very gesture that defined it spatially, a process that begins by construing the space of the other as "territory," a potential extension of the dominant space, something that can be mapped and, therefore, entered. The word fetish is a part of mapping. It is used at the borders to outline the unmappable, the strangest, least comprehensible symptoms of the other, that which makes the other truly other, bracketing it in order that the rest of the map can be completed. More than merely an agent of mapping, the word makes the map possible. The fetish is actively involved in the production of space.

Even though the fetish only exists in scenes of translation between radically different systems, it does not simply occupy those sites. It cannot simply be placed within the spaces that it defines. Rather, the fetish circulates in another economy of exchange between these very scenes of translation. Passed from scene to scene, it is produced by its own history of translation. As Pietz puts it, the fetish is "a radically historical object that is nothing other than the totalized series of its particular uses."[2] Consequently, the question of the fetish in architecture becomes: How might architecture participate in this series? Which contracts would have to be signed? In which ways is it already participating? To which extent is the series made possible by that participation?

Such questions do not involve merely applying the concept of the fetish to architecture by describing as "fetishistic" the appropriation of architectural objects by some psychosexual subject or describing the recent commodification of architectural discourse itself into a marketable object for mass consumption. It cannot be a matter of treating architecture as an object since precisely what

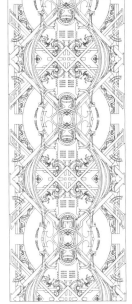

1. Ashanti Fetish House.

1.

2.

2. Ashanti Fetish Doctor.

fetishism calls into question is the status of objects and, therefore, of discourse. Rather, it involves tracing both the constitutional role of the fetish in architectural theory and the role of architecture in theories of the fetish. After all, it is the status of theory that is at stake in the fetish.

What seems to be neglected in contemporary discussions of the different forms of fetishism is that in each case it presupposes not only a subject —the fetishist (or the collective subjectivity of a fetishistic culture)—in a particular relationship with an object, or, more precisely, a certain displacement of an object—the fetish—but also an observer of that subject—the theorist (whether the writer of travel accounts, analytical case notes, psychoanalytic

3.

3. Baltimore Fetish House.

4.

4. Manhattan Fetish Doctors.

essays, political-economic treatises, ethnographic records, catalogue essays, cultural criticism, or anthropological notes). Each scene only becomes fetishistic with the presence of the theorist. For the fetishist, by definition, the relationship is not fetishistic.[3] It is the theorist that constructs fetishism as a pathological encounter with the other. For the fetishist, the fetish object is not the vehicle for a mediation with the other but is the thing in itself. The fetish is only other to theory, the fetish is only a fetish in theory.

Influenced by the early travel accounts of Africa, the institutions of high theory have defined themselves in opposition to the fetish. Theory is promoted as the removal of fetishes in favor of things-in-themselves; theory's rationality

is established in the face of the irrationality of the fetish. The fetish is literally an object-relation standing in the place of theory. Its otherness is precisely the absence of a coherent theory that can describe it. Inasmuch as theory's preferred description of itself is architectural (a stable construction erected in a place defining that place4), the fetish literally stands in the place of this architectural fantasy. The fetish therefore cannot simply be architectural, it would speak of an-other architecture, displacing the stable architecture of philosophy's dreams.

But it would not be safe to assume that the use of the word fetish by theory is itself strictly theoretical and hence straightforwardly architectonic. The architecture of the opposition between theory and fetish may not be so stable. On the contrary, as Baudrillard argued in his early essay "Fetishism and Ideology," the word fetish marks the fetishism of theory itself. Fetish is a "dangerous" word that "turns against those who use it" by becoming itself a fetish that "ideologically countersigns the very system of values that it otherwise dislocates."[5] The concept tends to resist the very theory that employs it. Baudrillard condemns the uncritical use of the word as a pejorative term in socioeconomic theory, arguing that it reproduces, rather than critiques, ideology. He employs psychoanalytic concepts to demonstrate that critical theory's pathological differentiation of phenomena into binary oppositions of categories actually denies difference and thereby acts as a fetishistic substitute for analysis, consolidating the oppressive mechanisms it claims to critique. The concept of fetish conceals a repression that sustains an oppression. The covert politics of the traditional use of the term reproduce the very operations that it overtly condemns. The operations of the fetish are internalized in the structure of the very theory that identifies and critiques them.

Such a "danger" clearly exists in architectural theory. While the concept of the fetish might be used to analyze architecture's complicity in the oppressive mechanisms underpinning the contemporary economy of commodification, it might just as likely become the latest sign of that commodification (whether employed as a negative term within a traditional conception of "the political" or a positive term reinscribed in the discourse as part of a redefinition of the site of politics). To simply reject the fetish in architecture runs the risk of burying deeper certain secrets common to both the institution of architectural discourse and its criticism—hence the conservative role of much writing that advertises itself as political critique in architecture.

What such critiques share, and what indeed identifies them as "political," is their routine opposition to formalism understood as a dissimulating mask veiling the real means of production, a layer of fetishistic decoration,

whether the literal ornament applied to a building, the building as a kind of ornament applied to everyday life, or the other representational systems applied to buildings: the glossy journals, photographic images, advertisements, and even the rhetorical surfaces of architectural theory. The fetish is always understood as a surface effect that makes an object available for consumption and the seduction of such a surface economy is always opposed to the substantial structural and structuring properties of objects. Structure is identified with the material life of the subject while decoration is identified with an ideological domain of representation that can alienate the subject from that materiality. In architectural theory, the political has become identified with the critique of surface, where critique is itself already identified with the attempt to go behind or beneath the surface.

Such arguments and their limitations, produced by an uncritical appropriation of socioeconomic theory, are all too familiar, but in recent years this particular use of the word fetish has been mobilized as the basis of a new interdisciplinary formation, a scene of translation between concepts of architecture and social theory. Socioeconomic theory is beginning to appropriate architectural theory to form a discourse in which space is the privileged term. In this interstitial site between spatial and social theory, a certain exchange of ideas appears to be going on. A new intellectual economy has emerged and is rapidly being institutionalized. Indeed, space has become a master term sustaining a global project of theorization. But this exchange, like those within which the word fetish was first coined, involves the exploitation of one discourse by another to sustain the imperialism of a particular theory—ironically, a theory that defines itself as a critique of the contemporary equivalent of colonialist expansion, the unrelenting movement of global capital.

I am, of course, referring to the school of thought pioneered by Fredric Jameson's 1984 essay "Postmodernism or the Cultural Logic of Late Capitalism"[6] which Jameson has followed up with a string of essays focusing on the question of space. This influential essay has become central to the work of the geographer David Harvey, as exemplified in his 1989 *The Condition of Postmodernity*[7] which in turn has spawned books like Edward Soja's *Postmodern Geographies: The Reassertion of Space in Critical Social Theory.*[8] All of these texts develop general social theories on the basis of a critique of what is argued to be the historically specific spatial condition of postmodernity. The use of both explicit and implicit concepts of space in each needs to be interrogated in more detail than is possible here but as Harvey's book is the most representative of the institutional discourse that has rapidly grown up around this line of enquiry, I will focus on it to outline the course of such an extended reading, a

reading that becomes increasingly urgent given recent developments in the political economy of theory itself.

HE POLITICS OF SURFACE

Harvey's elaborate criticism of postmodernism comes down to a simple critique of surface. He condemns the contemporary environment of "ornamentation," "embellishment," "accessories," and "decoration" and the resulting "diversification of surfaces" exemplified in the surfaces of postmodern buildings whose "theatricality of effect" is "not realism but a facade." The dissimulating facade of buildings become emblematic of the postmodern condition and is denounced as a form of fetishism. Describing the "contrived depthlessness" that Jameson's essay identified in postmodern space as "*the* overwhelming motif in postmodernism,"[9] Harvey identifies this "evident fascination with surfaces"[10] as a rejection of modern architecture's concern with "inner meaning" or "underlying reality" in which space was "subservient to the construction of a social project"[11]:

> *Attention to surfaces has, of course, always been important to modernist thought and practice (particularly since the cubists), but it has always been paralleled by the kind of question . . . how can we build, represent, and attend to these surfaces with the requisite sympathy and seriousness in order to get behind them and identify essential meanings? Postmodernism, with its resignation to bottomless fragmentation and ephemerality, generally refuses to contemplate that question.*[12]

Postmodernism is seen to fetishistically abandon this social reality beyond the surface in favor of a "constructed vision," an "image projected to the outside," a "mythological construction" employed as a "mask" to "draw a veil over real geography through the construction of images."[13] Surfaces are strategically deployed to "disguise" the social reality identified with that geographical space. This space is seen to be, by unquestioned definition, beyond surface. A theory of it is necessarily a social theory that penetrates or peels off the dissimulating surfaces of the contemporary environment to unmask the "essential" social values hidden behind them in an age in which even such a "search for roots" tends to be transformed into an image.[14]

There are many problems with this account. Harvey's readings of specific spaces are invariably limited in symptomatic ways. Postmodern architecture actually tends to reestablish and emphasize a gap between its structure and the layers of decoration, presenting its surface as just that, a suspended surface. It is simplistic to denounce, as a dissimulating masquerade,

the postmodern addition of a decorative surface (to what is usually a generic modern building type) in which the gesture of addition is made thematic. It is too easy to describe that which identifies itself as a mask as a mask. Indeed, these literal masks are arguably the least masklike aspects of contemporary architecture. To condemn them takes at face value the pronouncements of the polemicists of the modern movement and forgets that the advertised "austerity" of modern buildings is itself a surface effect. Modern architecture wears the mask of the unmasked, as exemplified in its emblematic addition of a layer of white skin to represent nakedness. And even this representation of the absence of representation could only be read as such with the addition of layer upon layer of "modern" theory. The whole attempt to historicize the question of the ornamental surface and separate it from social reality, which again uncritically reproduces the canonic interpretation of the goals of modern architecture promoted by those layers of theory, is problematic. The history of architectural discourse is a history of attitudes toward ornament in which ornament is always tied to the practice, and even the possibility, of social life. Harvey employs a modernist history to condemn the way in which the modern was displaced by the postmodern without making clear what precisely, in architecture anyway, has changed. The complexity of his account of the machinations of global capital is never matched by the account of the spaces said to exemplify it.

But the concern here is not so much the inadequacy of Harvey's arguments about architecture as the particular loading that they are given in his text, the kind of influence they have on the general position being advanced and its institutional success in spite of, or perhaps because of, their flaws.

Harvey's critique of the fetishism of masks is an extraordinarily literal reading of Marx. As he puts it, "Money and market exchange draws a veil over, 'masks' social relationships between things. This condition Marx calls 'the fetishism of commodities.'"[15] This socioeconomic concept is about surface before Harvey applies it to particular surfaces. He describes fetishism as the "direct concern with surface appearances that conceal underlying readings,"[16] and what is concealed is, of course, a base: the "real basis of economic distinctions," the "hidden" social conditions that "lie behind" the "real but nevertheless superficial relationships"[17] of the market. Metaphorically, the erection of a solid structure upon a base is opposed to the application of a thin facade meant to conceal that base. But just as this facade becomes literally the facade of a contemporary building in Harvey's text, the base becomes literally the spatial base of the built environment. The spatial structure clothed by those decorative surfaces is described as the "material base" for social practice.

This literalizes what Baudrillard calls the "metaphor of fetishism." The concepts being applied to architecture were already formulated with specific reference to architecture. Marx presented his account of the commodity fetish parallel to the infamous metaphor of base and superstructure.[18] The fetish is a superstructural substitution veiling the condition of the economic base, an "attachment" masking the material conditions of production. In this substitution of object relations for social relations, the fetish object not only assumes subjectivity but becomes master, actively producing rather than simply acting upon the alienated subject as such: "The objective conditions essential to the realization of labor are alienated from the worker and become manifest as fetishes endowed with a will and a soul of their own. Commodities in short, appear as the purchasers of persons."[19]

Harvey adopts this sense of alienation and applies it to the objects that occupy and define contemporary space. But for Marx, fetishism is not an inherent property of objects or of physical attachments to them. Rather, fetishism is itself the attachment. It is a form of mystification "attached" to an object like an applied superstructure maintaining the "secret" of structural alienation: "I call this the fetishism that *attaches* itself to the products of labor as soon as they are produced as commodities and is therefore inseparable from the production of commodities."[20] Fetishism is the attachment that transforms a physical form into a commodity. In the "social relation veiled beneath a material shell"[21] it is not the material shell as such, the fetish as a physical object, that is the veil but the fetishism attached to it and transforming it into a social agent that literally has a life of its own.

Significantly, Marx does not describe this fetishistic attachment to objects simply as the action of a deluded consumer. Rather, it is firstly the action of the theorist—the political economist—who identifies economic categories as formal properties of objects.[22] Himself such a theorist, Harvey reproduces the very operations that he condemns. In identifying the physical surface as the fetish, he fetishizes that surface, giving it the very social agency that he argues that it masks. Likewise, he takes the physical condition of objects, their capacity to function and structure, as a given and identifies it with the essential material base rather than as itself an ideological effect requiring critique.

But as with all rejections of fetishism (and all such appeals to the metaphor of architecture), these slips involve more than theoretical lapses. On the contrary, they sustain a particular concept of theory itself. The postmodernist's fetishistic celebration of "masking and cover up" is seen as a denial of the traditional role of an overarching theory able to go beyond the

surface.[23] For Harvey, the rejection of fetishism is necessarily linked to the constitution of a master theory: "Marx's meta-theory seeks to tear away that fetishistic mask, and to understand the social relations that lie behind it."[24] This theory is then opposed to the theories of postmodernism or, rather, theories seen to be postmodern inasmuch as they deny any particular theory a totalizing authority. Such theories are themselves understood as fetishistic surface plays, theoretical masks operating energetically on the surface to maintain "political silence." Throughout his book Harvey responds to what he sees as the threat that the postmodern fetishism of surface poses to the traditional status of theory.

But it is important to note that this rejection of surface is written into the rhetoric of Harvey's theory before concepts like fetishism are introduced. Harvey describes himself as rejecting a "surface" account of postmodernism, attempting to go "*behind* all this eclecticism" to reveal its "*deep* limitations" and "*superficial* advantages"[my italics]. This general concept of theory as that which goes beyond surface is seen to precede the strategic articulation of specific concepts like fetishism. In this sense, the explicit reference to fetishism is actually superfluous to the theory that makes it.

So too is the explicit reference to architecture. In Harvey's hands Marx's meta-theory does not rethink itself in its attempt to comprehend actual contemporary spaces. Rather, it invokes a traditional image of space in order to mobilize a new discursive formation to the authoritarian ends of a master theory. Architectural space appears to be investigated but in fact is left largely untouched. Despite his overt rejection of any single sense of space, Harvey preserves a single traditional description of space, neglecting the multiplicity of theories of space constituting architectural discourse, just as he neglects to discuss the geographically, economically, racially, gender and sexuality specific forms of resistance to the expansion of global capital against which his book claims to set itself.[25] The success of his discursive formation is intimately tied to that of the economy that it appears to critique.

In failing to address either political or spatial forms of resistance, the promised exchange between spatial and social theory does not occur. Space is appealed to more to sustain a particular social theory than to reread space. This theory is mobilized by the use of the traditional architectural metaphor but is catapulted into institutional success when that metaphor is literally applied to particular spaces. A self-proclaimed master theory is launched on the back of the question of space. In this way, an appeal to space is used to recover the traditional pretension of theory to distinguish between "truth, authority and rhetorical seductiveness."[26]

And it is literally seduction that is set up in opposition to theory: the theorist is the one able to resist seduction. The rejection of surface effects, like the whole tradition of such rejections around which the western tradition of theory has organized itself, is tacitly understood as the control of sexual desire. Harvey condemns "an architecture of spectacle, with its sense of surface glitter and transitory pleasure, of display and ephemerality, of jouissance,"[27] which is identified with "orgasmic effect,"[28] "pleasure, leisure, seduction and erotic life . . . lust, greed and desire."[29] Of course, all of these terms are traditionally applied to the artifact "woman," the culturally constructed figure of both sexuality and surface. Indeed, Harvey introduces his critique with a rejection of feminist artwork. The book begins by identifying the postmodern city's theatrical "malleability of appearances and surfaces"[30] (which it opposes to Le Corbusier's modern city) with Cindy Sherman's photographs, which later become his paradigm of the dangers of fetishistic masking:

> [Marx] would surely accuse those postmodernists who proclaim the 'impenetrability' of the 'other' as their creed, of overt complicity with the fact of fetishism and of indifference towards underlying social meaning. The interest in Cindy Sherman's photographs (or any postmodern novel for that matter) is that they focus on masks without commenting directly on social meanings over than on the activity of masking itself.[31]

The phallic pretension of this desire to penetrate the other organizes all the discourses that identify fetishism only in order to reject it and is already written into Marx: "Hence its fetish character is still relatively easy to penetrate."[32] But more than this, the text goes out of its way to illustrate postmodernism with images of naked women. David Salle's *Tight as a House*, a sketch of a clothed man juxtaposed on a painting of a woman's naked body, is surprisingly but symptomatically used to illustrate "the collision and super-imposition of different ontological worlds."[33] Likewise, Titian's nude The *Venus d'Urbino* is shown followed by Manet's modernist reworking of it in *Olympia* and Rauschenberg's postmodern elaboration in *Persimmon*. Finally,

5.

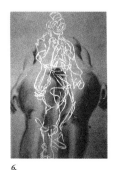

6.

7.

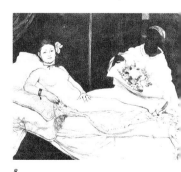

8.

an advertisement for Citizen Watches, a photograph of a naked woman overlaid with the advertising copy, is used to illustrate "the postmodernist techniques of superimposition of ontologically different worlds that bear no necessary relation to each other."[34] This raises the question: What is the necessary relation between the images of naked, or more precisely, tattooed, women that Harvey uses and his argument? Significantly, these images lead into the images of postmodern buildings that dominate the rest of the text. The eroticized surface of the woman's body is tacitly identified with the surfaces of buildings being condemned, in a book whose anxiety is all too symptomatically displayed on its cover which shows a woman breaking (out of) a skyscraper.

This rejection of both the feminine surface and feminist discourse is not a contingent event. It is not an oversight that can be corrected in order to recuperate or improve the theory; it is the very possibility of the theory as such. In order to produce a "master" theory, paradigmatic difference and theories of difference, especially feminist theories, must be effaced. These theories are necessarily theories of the surface that call the text's whole project into question.

In his attempt to get to the politics beyond the surface, Harvey neglects the politics of the surface itself, and particularly the politics of his own rhetoric, the surface effects his text employs. He exempts his text from its own critique. In so doing, his attempt to get beyond the fetish becomes itself fetishistic. As Rosalyn Deutsche argues:

> *Harvey, ignorant of contemporary materialist discourses about images and blind to the fact that some of the art he criticizes contests the fetishistic representation of woman, argues—in the name of anti-fetishism—for seemingly transparent images that reveal "essential" meanings. This—truly fetishistic—conception in which representations are produced by subjects who discover, rather than project, that meaning corresponds to Harvey's own image of society: a meta-theory that purports to perceive the single, absolute foundation of social coherence. Postmodernism interferes with that depiction.*[35]

10.   *11.*   *12.*

While many feminist discourses employ the concept of fetishism critically, most do not simply discard the surface they theorize. On the contrary, they elaborate strategies by which the construction of woman as the paradigmatic fetish object available for consumption by the masculine gaze can be turned against itself into the possibility of a radical critique, if not the production of the traditionally excluded female spectator position. Such strategies of resistance, and the associated theories of representation with which Harvey symptomatically fails to engage, locate the political in the production of surface. The question becomes: Which politics? Which surface? For whom?

As secrets are written into the surface itself rather than behind it, the simplistic rejection of surface in favor of structure needs to be replaced with an understanding of the structural role of the surface. Following Baudrillard's essay, this would imply the need to analyze the specific effects of the binary oppositions in architectural discourse that repress the real oppressions operative within, and dependant on, the economy of that discourse.

THE STRUCTURAL FETISH

But before deconstructing both the psycho-sexual and socio-economic politics of architectural theory, it needs to be understood that the "danger" of the word *fetish* that Baudrillard describes in his attempt to link Marxist and Freudian discourses is itself already architectural. Baudrillard's argument depends upon an architectural argument written into the rhetoric of his text but never made explicit as such nor, even less, subjected to the critical rigor of that text.

First, the essay describes the operations of the word *fetish* in architectural terms. Theory constructs itself through a process of mystification that, ironically, takes the form of the rejection of mystification of which fetishism acts as the paradigm. The fetish is a "metaphor" with which traditional theory "props itself up." It is a prop, a secondary structure on which the main structure depends. The metaphor "*shores up* magical thinking" in order to produce a "static," "secure," "restricted," "circumscribed," "encompassed" space: a "perfect closure effected by signs." It sustains a theoretical structure that defines some kind of place. But this structural prop is not simply behind the scenes. On the contrary, theoretical references to fetishism (and references to it, I would argue, can only be theoretical) act as a "facade" veiling the "structure" of the theory that erects it, blocking actual theoretical work in the name of theory. The structure or, rather, the politically strategic illusion of structure is held up and together by what appears to be added to it.

More than this, Baudrillard argues that the facade established by the concept of fetish is constructed by "the *fetishistic* theory of infrastructure and superstructure"[36] that privileges material structure over its supplements. What appears to be added to the structure of theory but makes that structure possible is the claim that what is added to any structure is necessarily subordinate to it. The use of the word *fetish* is therefore a facade sustained by the very distinction between facade and structure that is itself implicitly "fetishistic." The facade of theory is a certain theory of the facade: the theory that theory is that which goes beyond facades.

Baudrillard argues that if theoretical work involves going behind facades to locate the structures they veil then psychoanalysis is the only field that does not employ the term *fetish* fetishistically because it identifies the structural role of the fetish—which is to say that the only theory of the fetish is psychoanalytic. But clearly this or any "going behind" cannot be straightforward. The Freudian structure of the fetish is a "perverse structure" because the fetish endlessly complicates the distinction between facade and structure. The fetish destabilizes the very structure that it at once supplements and makes possible. It is in these architectural terms that Baudrillard's central attempt to exemplify his argument by destabilizing the traditional opposition between body and clothing (such that the body itself becomes a form of clothing) should be understood.

This instability is written into the etymology of the word fetish with which Baudrillard begins the essay. The clothing of the body is etymologically associated with the ornamentation of a building. But equally, it is etymologically associated with construction. The word fetish carries the senses of "fabrication," "making," "artifice," "cosmetics," "makeup," "adornment," and "embellishment." This chain carries both the sense of ornamentation and structure. The word participates in a series of words that combine these senses of ornamental clothing and construction. "Fashion," for example, can mean both the ephemeral surface and to make. "Fabricate" is both to dissimulate and to build. And even the word facade itself emerges from facere (to make). The fetish, by definition, convolutes the distinction between structure and ornament.

This double sense is unwittingly invoked by Harvey's references to the "construction of images," "image construction," "image building," etc., undermining his overall attempt to separate decorative image from structure and complicating his final attempt to dismiss postmodern architecture by making the routine identification of its developers with fashion conscious clothing manufacturers.

It is precisely through the figure of clothing that the image can be understood as the possibility of spatial structure rather than simply its disguise. Architectural theories propounding this argument could be elaborated in order to understand better both contemporary spatiality and contemporary theory.[37] But the link between clothing and construction is not exploited by Baudrillard. While he develops his etymological argument at length by demonstrating the ways in which the body is itself a form of clothing, the structure/ornament opposition remains unexamined. Whereas clothing is treated as the privileged "illustration" or "example" of the argument, architecture is understood as but an organizational metaphor, applied to the presentation of the argument rather than to its ostensible subject: fetishism. Having identified the convolution of structure and ornament as the very mechanism of the theoretical fetish, Baudrillard restores and employs the same opposition to organize theory, reconstituting theory as that which goes behind facades, albeit to identify a "perverse structure." He sustains a simple distinction between theoretical work and ideological reproduction that must itself be called into question by the perverse architecture of the fetish that he has already identified.

An architectural argument or, more precisely, a disruption of the generic image of architecture that underwrites traditional theory makes Baudrillard's central thesis possible, but as the text progresses it is increasingly and simultaneously displaced both into the generic form it has been used to destabilize and into a metaphor that can be separated from the main body of the argument and therefore left uninterrogated. Indeed, Baudrillard's text attains its own status as "theory" by rehearsing this classical gesture of making architecture a metaphor.

This gesture has to be understood in terms of the essay's place in the development of Baudrillard's work whose changing relationship to ornamental surface marks the changes in its politics. The essay lies between the early work, which constructs itself as orthodox theory in order to offer a conventional materialist critique of the products of mass consumption whose "structure is invaded by astructural elements," ornamental disguises that produce a "cancer of the object,"[38] and the late work which attempts to reduce its allegiances to high theory and celebrates the dominance of those decorative surfaces by oscillating wildly between euphoric bliss and nihilistic pessimism.[39] The essay exemplifies an ambivalence toward decoration that can be located within the earnest dogma of the other texts and in the end complicates both their declared and perceived political credentials. But the essay fails to exploit the capacity to redefine the political implicit in this

constitutional ambivalence by bracketing off the architectural concepts that it employs.

In order to reexamine the image of architecture that the essay in the end exempts from analysis in order to assume theoretical status, we need to examine its role in the psychoanalytic tradition, which is also exempted from critique because it is said to be the only theory that has identified the underlying structure in which the fetish should be placed, "returning fetishism to its context within a perverse *structure* that perhaps underlies all desire."[40] Likewise, Pietz argues that psychoanalysis is the only discourse within which the term fetish has a "proper" place, becoming, for the first time, "an institutionally defined object within a particular culture or social order."[41] That is to say, it becomes a discrete classifiable object in a field, an object available to theory—an object only inasmuch as it is theorized.

The question here becomes: If the perverse architecture of the fetish problematizes the institution of theory that defines itself as architectonic inasmuch as it excludes the fetish, what is the architecture written into the theory that accommodates the fetish by identifying its perverse structure?

THE ARCHITECTURE BEHIND THE COUCH

Freud's account of fetishism is explicitly architectural. The fetish is a "construction" erected in order to maintain a secret by being "set up" in the "place" of something else. The question of the fetish is first and foremost a question of place. Fetishistic disavowal of the traumatic perception of the woman's lack of a penis has "taken place" when a substitute "has taken the place of" or "replaced," the maternal phallus through the mechanism of "displacement." The fetish only exists as such when it both occupies and veils a space not properly its own. In this psychic topography, the structure of the fetish cannot be separated from the displacement that it effects.[42] The concept of fetish involves a particular conflation of structure and place.

But this is a strange architecture. The "ground" on which the fetish is erected is an unresolvable, abysmal conflict between the avowal and disavowal of a loss. The unique attitude of the fetishist is to both acknowledge and deny the absence of the woman's penis and, therefore, of sexual difference. This rupturing of the ground is also a disruption of the definition of place. The conflict radically convolutes the topographical distinction between inside and outside, splitting the ego which mediates between the "interiority" of the id

and the "exterior" world. Erected on and by conflicting propositions, the architecture of the fetish disrupts the traditional architectonic fantasies of both structure and place.

This inscription of the psyche in spatial terms seems unproblematically metaphorical. Indeed, Freud explicitly warns against reading the metaphor too literally. He appears to employ it contingently like so many other notorious figures (thermodynamic, electrical, writing, photographic, mechanical . . . etc.), but this in no way reduces its strategic importance. On the contrary the issue becomes: When is this particular metaphor employed? In which situations does it invariably present itself? Which arguments cannot be made without this insignificant supplement?

These questions are further complicated when dealing with Freud's arguments about fetishism inasmuch as he identifies the fetish's disruption of the psychic topography with a literal space occupied by physical objects. In order not to face an unthinkable gap in an object (paradigmatically, the absence of a penis on the woman's body), an absence that calls into question its objecthood, its capacity to present itself, literally to erect itself, the fetishist focuses on a substitute [ersatz] "attached" to it, an adjacent supplement (typically, an item of clothing close to the surface of the body or the body's own clothing—hair—or parts of the body such as "attached" to the sexual organs). This accessory is then "detached" to become the sole object of interest. The detour becomes the end. The ersatz becomes the satz. The fetish is, by definition, a kind of ornament that assumes the role and status of the structure to which it is added.

But the detachment is not complete. The ornament never simply becomes structural. Rather, the distinction between ornament and structure is endlessly confused, undecidably complicated. The status of the substitute as such is both affirmed and denied. It oscillates between structure and ornament, between masking the original object and marking it, between belonging to and intruding on a space, between standing on its own and being a prop. Even the original structure it stands in for is itself a substitute. At the end of the essay entitled "Fetishism," Freud suddenly announces that the penis, the paradigm of presence, erection and structure, is itself a fetish, a nonstructural supplement: "In conclusion we may say that the normal prototype of fetishes is a man's penis."[43] Its supplementarity is even written into the inefficiency of the expression "man's penis."

This literal architecture of the fetish cannot simply be separated from the apparently metaphorical psychic architecture of fetishism. In Freud, as in Marx, fetishism, like the fetish object, is itself an "attachment." The incomplete "detachment" of the fetish from the original object of attention is identified

with the incomplete "detachment" of the ego from reality. Clearly, this identification of the constituted subject with the constitution of objects (already effected by describing the psyche in spatial terms) is itself fetishistic, if not paradigmatically so. The theorist here identifies certain apparently architectural properties of objects (like the supplementary role of ornamental surfaces) with the psychic condition of a patient. In Freud's text the architectural metaphor operates as a kind of fetish, a detour that constantly returns, marking and remarking a scene within which there is a series of overlapping identifications between object, subject, analyst, and theorist. This ersatz architecture disrupts not only the status of subject and object and the privileged relationship between them but also the relationship between analysis and theory.

In the late essay "Constructions in Analysis" for example, Freud describes the process of analysis in explicitly architectural terms:

> [The analyst's] task is to make out of what has been forgotten from the traces which it has left behind or, more correctly, to construct it. . . . His work of construction, or, if it is preferred, of reconstruction, resembles to a great extent an archaeologist's excavation of some dwelling-place that has been destroyed and buried or of some ancient edifice. The two processes are in fact identical. . . . But just as the archaeologist builds up the walls of the building from the foundations that have remained standing, determines the number and position of the columns from depressions in the floor and reconstructs the mural decorations and paintings from the remains found in the debris, so does the analyst proceed when he draws his inferences from the fragments of memories, from the associations and from the behavior of the subject of the analysis. Both of them have an undisputed right to reconstruct by means of supplementing and combining the surviving remains.[44]

But Freud immediately attempts to limit this metaphor. The constructions of the analyst are not like literal architecture because although pieces of the psychic structure are never simply lost, as they can be from buildings, they are always buried deeper such that the structure always remains mysterious: "psychical objects are incomparably more complicated than the excavator's material ones and . . . their finer structure contains so much that is mysterious."[45] The psychic base upon which the analyst builds is never secure. The "supplements" that the analyst adds to the exposed structure always sit upon certain gaps in that structure. And also, "the comparison can go no further than this" because the analyst's work on the structure does not simply precede that of its decoration. The two occur together in a kind of dialectical

exchange. As this does not seem to make sense in architecture, the metaphor has to be detached from the main body of the argument that it has helped to launch.

But in the very gesture of abandoning the metaphor, Freud redeploys it in a different form. Whereas originally the analyst's constructions significantly included the "mural decorations and paintings" attached to the edifice that is the patient's psyche and form an important part of that psyche, the "internal decoration of the rooms" now refers both to the patient's responses to the analyst's construction and to the constructions themselves:

> [construction] is not however, a preliminary labor in the sense that the whole of it must be completed before the next piece of work can begin, as, for instance, is the case with house-building, where all the walls must be erected and all the windows inserted before the internal decoration of the rooms can be taken in hand. Every analyst knows that things happen differently in an analytic treatment and that there both kinds of work are carried on side by side, the one kind being always a little ahead and the other following behind it. The analyst finishes a piece of construction and communicates it to the subject of the analysis so that it may work upon him; he then constructs a further piece out of the fresh material pouring in on him, deals with it in the same way and proceeds in this alternating fashion until the end.[46]

The architectural metaphor is used here to identify its own limitation. The analyst supplements the material offered by the patient by building upon it a "construction," but that supplement then produces more material that may or may not support its structure, that is itself a fantasy about the structure that might lie behind the surface of that material. The roles of structure and decoration endlessly flip between patient and analyst, and with each turn the decoration becomes structural. This ambivalent oscillation between decoration and structure that is so paradigmatic of both the analytical scene and the individual psyche is, for Freud, inconceivable in architecture. "False constructions" play a strategic role in the production of analytical and psychic edifices in a way that seems prohibited in actual buildings.[47]

Despite this, the metaphor never simply goes away from this or from any of Freud's texts. Indeed, they describe themselves with it. Freud presents the construction of his theory in architectural terms. In the final section of the late *Outline of Psychoanalysis*, entitled "The Theoretical Yield," psychoanalytic theory is described as a "construction" involving the laying down of a "hypothesis" to establish "foundations" that are "supplemented, built on to" with further propositions, gradually "building up" a position.[48]

While this appears to reinforce the traditional architectonic fantasy of theory, from the 1914 essay "On Narcissism"onward (as Samuel Weber argues) Freud repeatedly attempts to distinguish the condition of psychoanalytic theory from this fantasy which he identifies with speculative philosophy.[49] Just as the analyst assembles constructions on an irreducibly mysterious base, the theory of psychoanalysis is "erected upon" a certain obscurity rather than on a "smooth, logically unassailable foundation" like philosophy. While philosophy is concerned with "filling in gaps,"[50] psychoanalysis is founded upon such gaps. Its "basic concepts" are "not the foundation-stone but the top of the whole structure and they can be replaced and discarded without damaging it."[51] That which is most "basic" is still supplementary. The structure is literally built out of ornaments. Psychoanalytic theory is a series of supplements to original observations that unlike the logical premises of philosophy, are always partially blocked. A certain blindness is, as it were, "built into" observation. The theoretical edifice is constructed upon certain gaps. Consequently, a fundamental relationship exists between the construction of psychoanalytic theory and the way in which the analyst builds up a construction.

This strange architecture, in turn, is entangled with that of the psyche. The initial hypothesis on which psychoanalytic theory was based—of "a psychical apparatus extended in space"[52]—"gives rise" to a general theory of the psyche. Both the model of theory in general as an erection and the specific hypothesis on which that theory is based are spatial. The form of theory (construction) cannot simply be separated from what it describes (the psyche as a spatial construction). The edifice of the psyche emerges from the child's construction of "theories"[53] which are "delusions" like those of the architectonic fantasy of high theory. Through a kind of countertransference, this type of delusion is not just examined but reproduced in analysis. Freud ends the essay "Constructions in Analysis" by suddenly announcing that the analyst's constructions have the same form as the patient's delusions: "I have not been able to resist the seduction of an analogy. The delusions of patients appear to me the equivalents of the constructions which we build up in the course of an analytic treatment." [54]

It must be remembered that Freud's theory presents itself as emerging from analyses of specific patients, beginning of course with his self-analysis in which patient, analyst, and theorist are one. This primal identification returns throughout the later texts such that psychoanalytic theory can be said to have internalized the very pathologies that it identifies. To explain the way the analyst's constructions resemble the delusions of the patient, Freud

employs the concept of "disavowal" that he had first introduced to explain fetishism.[55] And indeed, in each case (patient, analyst, theorist) the spatial structure is that of fetishism itself, the supplementation of a gap in which the substitute becomes the real thing, the "false construction" becomes the structure.

One of the fulcrums of this countertransference is the word *satz* written into the *ersatz* condition of the fetish and meaning at once thesis–proposition and position–place. This slippage between theory and space makes possible the transference between psychoanalytic theory and the subjectivity of the fetishist whereby theory becomes the manufacture of supplementary propositions that assume the structural role of the flawed construction to which they are added in order to maintain certain secrets about that structure in the face of unresolvable conflict. Just as the child struggles to sustain its early theories about sexuality by supplementing them in the face of evidence that would destroy them, the theory of psychoanalysis sustains itself with supplements in the face of the symptoms that it cannot rationalize.

ETISHIZING FETISHISM

One such ersatz building block is the concept of fetishism itself, which emerges in the face of what Freud variously describes as the "riddle," "secret," "enigma," and "puzzle" of the fetishist's symptoms. If, as Pietz and Baudrillard argue, the fetish only assumes a proper place within psychoanalysis, it significantly only appears as a self-sufficient topic in Freud's extremely short essay of 1927 entitled "Fetishism," framed by its brief introduction in the early Three Essays on the Theory of Sexuality (1905) and its concluding summary in the late Outline of Psychoanalysis (1940). Like all fetishes, it appears to be added as a "detour" from the main thesis, a deviation to illustrate arguments over which it holds no special claim: "It must not be thought that fetishism presents an exceptional case. . . . It is merely a favorable subject for studying the question. Let us return to the thesis."[56] The thesis in this case is the concept of repression that Freud elsewhere describes as the "foundation–stone" of psychoanalytic theory. But, as with any fetish, such a return is not possible. The prosthetic illustration permanently displaces the theory to which it is attached.

Having originally stated in *Three Essays on the Theory of Sexuality* that fetishism can be explained with the "oldest" terms of psychoanalysis, Freud later argues that it requires a new terminology of "disavowal" that necessarily transforms the theory that employs it. The word refers to the undecidable

structure of the fetish established by the "double attitude" of the fetishist—"he retains this belief but also he gives it up"[57]—which necessarily splits the psychic topography. The concept of the splitting of the ego, which becomes central to the final accounts of psychoanalysis and dominates the late essays,[58] is first articulated in detail in the essay on fetishism and is always explained with examples of fetishism.

In this way, fetishism, the unexceptional "supplement" that "as a rule . . . made its appearance in analysis as a subsidiary finding,"[59] is the special case that focuses attention on the unresolvable structural conflicts between contrary attitudes resulting from all forms of ego defense against the internal and external worlds. Just as the fetish is, by definition, an ornament made structural, the ornamental question of the fetish actually organizes the theory to which it is added.

But even more than this, the question of fetishism is a significant part of the production of the theory of infantile sexuality to which it appears to be added and by which it is, in turn, explained. As Alan Bass argues, Freud's account of fetishism emerged out of his extended reading of Leonardo, which began during the time of his self-analysis in the late 1890s (and continued to be a form of self-analysis inasmuch as Freud identified with Leonardo) and cannot be separated from the crucial revision of his thinking about infantile sexuality and hence psychoanalytic theory in general.[60]

Freud's theory that the child is itself a theorist, elaborating supplementary constructions to both rationalize and cover over its observations, of which the "first" such theory is that of the maternal penis, literally emerged during his own observations of the case of Leonardo (which he would later identify as a case of fetishism[61]), before he analyzed fetishism in terms of the child's first theory. Freud's 1908 essay "On the Sexual Theories of Children" which, as his letters reveal, is entangled with the study of Leonardo,[62] marks the first identification of the psychic importance of the penis and the child's theory that the mother possesses one and the first appearance of the expression "castration complex" as well as the elaboration of its centrality in the organization of the psyche. It is therefore, to extend Bass's argument, not just the concept of disavowal that emerges from the question of fetishism but even the fundamental concept of the centrality of the penis and consequently the whole edifice of the psyche and, in turn, psychoanalysis, "constructed" around the fear of its loss. Indeed, the castration complex that preserves the child's first theories is later described in terms of disavowal.[63]

Freud's capacity, like the child's, to produce theory is therefore at least doubly bound to the question of fetishism, such that, as Bass argues, the

theory becomes itself fetishistic according the "mutual complication of transference and theoretical advance that is so intrinsic to the history of
psychoanalysis."[64]

But while it is possible to trace the way in which the theoretical
ornament of fetishism structures Freudian theory, this is resisted by the texts.
By the time of the "Fetishism" essay, the only sign of fetishism's constitutional
role is that it is offered as the best evidence for the existence of the castration
complex: "Investigations into fetishism are to be recommended to all who
still doubt the existence of the castration complex . . . ."[65] The structural role
of the concept is never acknowledged. Indeed, in his postscript to An
Autobiographical Study (1935), Freud describes his work on fetishism as "an
important piece of analytical work" but one "either unessential or would soon
have been supplied by someone else."[66] To insist that the question of fetishism
is an inessential supplement is, of course, symptomatic. Just as the traumatic
sight of the absence of the penis, which can only be accommodated with the
construction of a fetish, is described by Freud as "uncanny,"[67] his own
encounter with fetishism, which can only be accommodated by reconstruct-
ing psychoanalytic theory, is itself uncanny, if not traumatic. Fetishism is the
"strange" condition that is somehow all too familiar. Hence Freud's simultaneous denial and affirmation of the need for new terms to describe it:

> Now a term is justified when it describes a new fact or brings it into
> prominence. There is nothing of that kind here; the oldest word in our
> psychological terminology, "repression," already refers to this pathological
> process. If we wish to differentiate between what happens to the idea as
> distinct from the affect, we can restrict "repression" to relate to the affect;
> the correct word for what happens to the idea is then "denial." [68]

This ambivalence is sustained by An Outline of Psychoanalysis precisely when it begins to generalize the mechanisms of the specific case of
fetishism—"Disavowals of this kind occur very often and not only with
fetishists . . . . The facts of this splitting of the ego . . . are neither so new nor
so strange as they may first appear"[69]—and forms the opening of his unfinished, and posthumously published, essay "On the Splitting of the Ego": "I
find myself for a moment in the interesting position of not knowing whether
what I have to say should be regarded as something long familiar and obvious
or as something entirely new and puzzling. But I am inclined to think the
latter."[70]

The uncanny authority of the undecidable structure of the fetish haunts
psychoanalytic theory. The concept cannot be easily placed in the edifice it

organizes. Freud has as much difficulty placing it within the final *An Outline of Psychoanalysis* as he did in *Three Essays on the Theory of Sexuality*. When addressing the question for the first time in the earlier text, he exemplifies the paradigmatic confusion of the fetishist in being unsure whether to place it in the section devoted to deviations of the subject's aim or deviations in the object.[71]

Precisely because it has what is described by Lacan as a "special place" and by Karl Abraham as a "unique position" in Freud's account of sexuality, fetishism cannot be placed by the theory that it covertly produces and supposedly exemplifies.[72] It is a supplement added to an already flawed, and irreducibly mysterious theoretical structure that transforms that structure without being able to simply occupy it. While Freud repeatedly defends psychoanalytic theory as such a strange construction assembled on observations organized by a certain blindness, his attempt to theorize fetishism pushes even this concept to the limit, as can be seen by the way he begins his first paper on fetishism, presented to the Vienna Psychoanalytic Society on February 24, 1909, the minutes of which only recently been rediscovered: "Departing from his principle not to formulate theory before it can be supported by observations, the speaker would like to communicate, by way of exception, a theory of fetishism which is based only on a small number of observations."[73]

This particular theory without a solid base, which ends by suggesting that its development would have "solved the riddle of fetishism,"[74] not only lacks "support" but becomes a good example of a "false construction" never simply abandoned. It elaborates the account of fetishism as the return of the repressed pleasure in smell from the anal period, which Freud would later appear to displace in favor of the account of fetishism as the substitution for the maternal penis.

Bass identifies the first documentation of the new theory as Freud's letter to Jung dated November 21 of the same year, which claims to have "hit upon what I hope is the ultimate secret of foot-fetishism,"[75] and its first publication as the second edition of the *Three Essays on the Theory of Sexuality* (1910) and the Leonardo study in April of the same year. The various editions of the *Three Essays* (which Freud rated, along with *The Interpretation of Dreams*, as his most important publication) reveal the successive additive modifications of its "theory." A supplementary footnote is added to the second edition to fill a "gap" in the basic theory. It begins by claiming that "psychoanalysis has cleared up one of the remaining gaps in our understanding of fetishism" and offers the "coprophilic pleasure in smelling" to account for it, to which is then

Mark Wigley

13.

appended the second theory: "Another factor that helps towards explaining the fetishistic preference for the foot is to be found among the sexual theories of children, the foot represents a women's penis."[76] Neither account is announced as a change of position. On the contrary, the first is but a supplementary footnote and the second is but a supplement of that supplement. In fact, Freud describes the many additions to the book as "supplements," "extensions" constituting not transformations of the

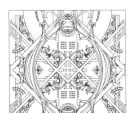

original theory of sexuality but "restorations" of it.[77] But the new theory of fetishism buried within the footnote had already begun to transform both this text and all of the other essays. It is responsible for the whole section "Sexual Theories of Children" added to the main body of the third edition (1915) and installs the castration complex at the center of the theory. By confining the source of that theory to an ornamental footnote, Freud symptomatically denies its structural role.

But despite this relentless attempt to marginalize fetishism, it ends up also occupying part of the center: "A certain degree of fetishism is thus habitually present in normal love."[78] For Freud, it is the most interesting "aberration" located within normal sexuality, the "variation" of the norm that appears most pathological, the "extension" of normal life that perverts that life. It is seen to pass from the normal to the pathological only when the fetish is "detached" from the legitimate object of sexual desire to which it was originally "attached"—that is, when the ornament fully takes the place of the object it appears to depend. The moment of perversion is therefore precisely the moment of a perversion of architecture.

Indeed, at first Freud might seem to place the fetish at the "borders of the pathological"[79] and maintain that border as the traditional gap between the attachment and detachment of ornament as part of his early attempt, started by the study of dreams, to "avoid the familiar reproach that we base our constructions of normal mental life on pathological grounds."[80] In the very gesture of subverting traditional thinking about architecture by identifying the structural role of supplements, Freud appears to recover the traditional architectonic of high theory. His own theory appears here to be separated from the psyche's false constructions, especially those of the fetishist. Fetishism is "placed" in the gaps between normal and pathological, variation and perversion, subject and object, structure and ornament, and inside and outside with which the institution of theory traditionally defines itself.

But it occupies these gaps in a way that at once bridges, maintains, and undermines this whole system of "theoretical" distinctions that psychoanalysis everywhere problematizes yet upon which it relies for its own authority as theory. Fetishism destabilizes the very conventions on which psychoanalysis necessarily erects itself precisely in order to then place them in doubt. Consequently, the way in which fetishism slips through all the attempts to frame it and maintains a certain restless mobility throughout the system plays a crucial, though again unacknowledged, role in Freud's general argument that the "disposition to perversions" is actually "a part of what passes as the normal

Mark Wigley

constitution."[81] Inasmuch as the difference between normal and pathological is, in the end, "conventional," one can finally abandon the architectonic fantasy necessary to other kinds of theory and understand "the normal life of the mind from a study of its disorders." Perversions, like fetishism, give access to the status of the ground supposedly lying under or behind the pathological: "The conclusion now presents itself to us that there is indeed something innate lying behind the perversions but that it is something innate in everyone . . . the constitutional roots of the sexual instinct."[82] Again, it is the false construction, the deviation, that gives access to the basic structure.

And again, the study of fetishism is not simply an example of this anti-architectonic principle but its exemplar. The ambivalence between normal and pathological is its very structure, as was written into the first canonic psychiatric use of the term to which Freud refers in his first paper on the subject: "The name fetishism originates with Ebing, who also stresses, absolutely correctly, that *just here* the transition from the normal to the pathological is very fluid"[83] [my italics].

But, more than offering a means of access to the condition of the normal psyche, fetishism becomes the model for the normal itself. The roots of sexuality are, of course, understood as a scene of unresolvable conflict. The ground on which the psyche is erected is permanently ruptured. It is itself perverse. The child is literally "polymorphously perverse" but its perversity is gradually repressed and this repression is even "as it were, extended into theory" when adults "disavow" the evidence of infantile sexuality.[84] High theory reproduces the fetishistic disavowal that sustains the child's theories and substitutes the evidence with a "disguise." In rejecting the content of those theories, that cannot be separated from their structure as theories, Freud relocates the "normal" somewhere between perversion and its repression. And like the fetishistic construction of high theory, the construction of the con-scious subject is no more than the consolidation of symptoms erected as "substitutes" that at once disguise and fulfill repressed wishes. The psyche is a fragile ensemble of substitute formations [*Ersatzbilding*], supplements that, in their endless repetition, literally structure the subject. In this sense, which Lacanian theory would later elaborate, the subject is produced by a certain fetishism. As Jacqueline Rose argues, "the structure of subjectivity . . . is in itself fetishistic."[85]

What is being excavated and reconstructed by the analyst is therefore not simply a building in which the structural base precedes the decoration but one in which the decoration is structural. The analyst is, after all, no more than a certain kind of a reader of decorative surfaces.

114

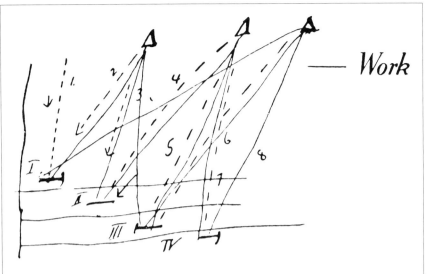

14.

HE PERVERSE ARCHITECTURE
OF THE PSYCHE

Significantly, Freud's account of symptoms is often explicitly architectural. An architectural rhetoric is employed to sustain the most basic concept of the symptom as a substitute formation, the "construction" of which cannot be separated from that of the subject. Throughout his work, Freud is concerned with the "construction of symptoms."[86] This metaphor becomes more pointed in the *Outline of Psychoanalysis*. When discussing the dream work as the model for the mechanism that produces symptoms and its interpretation, in turn, as the model for psychoanalysis, Freud describes the "compromise-structure" of the manifest content of the dream that substitutes for the latent content as a "*facade*." Symptoms, in general, are constructed as facades understood as thin surfaces disguising what is behind them.

This apparently passing architectural reference is but the end of a thread that can be traced back through Freud's texts. In the *New Introductory Lectures* (1933), for example, the role of secondary revision is described as filling in the gaps, the inconsistencies and illogic of the dream, in order to produce a "smooth facade that cannot fit its true content," such that if it is omitted the dream will "display all its rents and cracks openly."[87] If it is present, such gaps are smoothed over, disguised by the evasive ruses of condensation and displacement. Psychoanalysis operates on these gaps, whether disguised or not. When the earlier *Introductory Lectures on Psychanalysis* (1917) describes symptoms in terms of the manifest content of dreams, the architectural analogy is more detailed:

Mark Wigley

*Even if it has an apparently sensible exterior, we know that this has only
come out through dream distortion and can have as little organic relation
to the internal content as the facade of an Italian church has to its structure
and plan. There are other occasions when this facade has its meaning, and
reproduces an important component of the latent dream-thoughts with
little or no distortion. But we cannot know this before we have submitted
the dream to interpretation and have been able to form a judgement from
it as to the amount of distortion that has taken place.*[88]

This reference, in turn, can be traced back to an even more detailed
image in the canonic *Interpretation of Dreams* (1900) in which, when continuing the self-analysis with which psychoanalysis was founded, Freud
analyzes one of his own dreams, a dream that, significantly, he had in August
1898 at the beginning of his thinking on Leonardo. It is the dream that
produced the most material about his own infantile sexuality, material that
would only later be explicitly theorized in terms of the castration complex.
Freud describes his memory of this dream as being

*like the facade of an Italian church in having no organic relation with
the structure lying behind it. But it differed from those facades in being
disordered and full of gaps, and in the fact that portions of the interior
construction had forced their way through into it at many points.*[89]

The facade is no longer a seamless decorative screen independent from
and completely masking the structure of the interior. The incompletion of
secondary revision leaves gaps through which parts of the latent content "force
their way" but are still not simply visible. What is crucial here is that the interior
is never seen as such. The gaps in the facade make the latent content, with its
relentless drive to the surface, available, but, it can still only be seen within the
decorative layer through interpretations that might lead to constructions that
are always, in a certain sense, false. The analyst can only work on the surface,
"filling in" the gaps by locating the traces of the various displacements and
condensations, rebuilding the facade in order to reconstruct a sense of the
structure behind it.[90]

The strongest form of resistance to this work of analysis is "put up" by
transference which itself involves the ongoing maintenance, which is to say
(re)production, of a "facade." But this facade actually brings to the surface the
very material that it attempts to protect:

*Resistances of this kind [transference] should not be one-sidedly
condemned. They include so much of the most important material from
the patient's past and bring it back in so convincing a fashion that they
become some of the best supports of the analysis if a skilful technique knows*

how to give them the right turn. Nevertheless, it remains a remarkable fact that this material brings to the fore a facade that is hostile to the treatment. . . . Indeed we come finally to understand that the overcoming of these resistances is the essential function of analysis.[91]

Likewise, the facade of the dream attempts to veil its own construction as well as that of the latent content. In fact, for Freud, the essence of the dream is not the latent content but the dream work that constructs the facade, the mechanism that translates latent into manifest material. Psychoanalysis does not locate hidden content by applying well-known translating codes to the surface; rather it identifies the specific mechanism of translation that both constitutes and defends the psyche by ordering the texture of its surface. The secret is not hidden by the code but is the code. The essence of the dream is not the structure hidden by the facade but the structure of the facade itself.

This operation is further elaborated in the analysis of the joke work that Freud identifies closely with the dream work. Through the same mechanisms of condensation and displacement, the joke work produces a "facade" such that the technique of any joke is no more than the "construction of a facade." This "outer shell" or "mask" assumes its facade-like quality either through consistent ("cynical") or faulty ("comic") logic. The logical facade conceals faulty reasoning and the illogical facade conceals reasonable but prohibited claims. But the facade masks not only the unspoken structures presumed to lie behind it but its own masking. This sets up further convolutions of disguise. In this way, that which cannot normally be spoken "can only be made under the mask of a joke and indeed of a joke concealed by its facade"[92]:

> *But if a joke admits of this doubt [whether it is a joke] the reason can only be because it has a facade—in these instances a comic one—in the contemplation of which one person is satiated while another may try to peer behind it. A suspicion may arise, moreover, that his facade is intended to dazzle the examining eye and that these stories have therefore something to conceal. . . . thanks to their facade, they are in a position to conceal not only what they have to say but also the fact that they have something—forbidden—to say.*[93]

In this way, what cynical jokes actually disguise are cynicisms, rational but unspeakable indictments, and what comic jokes disguise are irrational desires. Both the "appearance of logic" and the "appearance of irrationality" veil prohibited logics and fulfill desires. The organization of the joke always turns on the tension between sound and faulty reasoning. The joke is literally produced in the juxtaposition of the structural and the nonstructural. Again,

the architectonic metaphor is subverted. The appearance of structure can be a facade, and the irrational facade can be structural. This double masquerade can also be seen in the analysis of the dream work, where an innocent facade tends to mask perverse desire while the perverse dream tends to mask innocence, unless the mechanism of censorship that produces the facade breaks down such that the perverse dream actually reveals a perverse desire.[94]

The analyst works only on such facades, always from the outside. Psychoanalysis presupposes and depends upon the structural role of the facade. The texture of this depthless surface of representation is produced by the repression of the interior "material" of the unconscious, with its drive to the surface, on the one hand, and the disavowal of the impact of the exterior world on the other. The facade is literally a line of resistance between inside and outside. It is the outer surface of the ego, whether or not it is split, that Freud repeatedly describes as a thin "layer." The psyche is a spatial projection from and on a surface.

RCHITECTURE AS THE FETISH OF THEORY

Freud everywhere seeks to differentiate his project and its objects from the collective understanding of architecture as a stable construction on a solid ground that is then decorated with a subordinate layer of decoration but he constantly returns to it, even while attempting to abandon it.

In fact, Freud attempts to detach the whole spatial metaphor from his theory but in so doing reinvokes it. When addressing "the theory which we had attempted to construct," he refers to the "topographical" account of the mind "being built up by a number of functional systems whose interrelations may be expressed in spatial terms" as but a "supplement" that can be abandoned. It is part of the "speculative superstructure" of psychoanalytic theory, unlike the concept of repression which is understood as the "founda-tion-stone," and that of infantile sexuality, which is laid upon it much later as the "theoretical-structure."[95] Again, the spatial metaphor is used to describe its own redundancy. It is retained to describe the condition of the theory itself while its potential removal from the content of that theory is announced.

The complications of this ambivalence about the metaphor can be seen more clearly when, in the *Introductory Lectures on Psychoanalysis*, Freud elaborates the topographical metaphor in extended detail in terms of the "crudest idea": rooms of a house and the relationships between them. The interior of the psyche becomes the interior of a house. But before, during and after this description Freud declares that this specific "picture," and in turn the general spatial model of the psyche such metaphors sustain, is unscientific. He

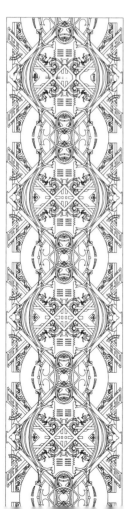

stresses the need to replace this supplement because it is detached from any observation. More than this, he announces that he already has a replacement for the spatial model. But he doesn't say what this replacement is and goes on to defend the original speculative image as a supplement needed in order to explain his observations. Again, he ends up giving the apparently ornamental supplement a structural role:

> *The crudest idea of these systems is the most convenient for us —a spatial one. Let us therefore compare the system of the unconscious to a large entrance hall, in which the mental impulses jostle one another like separate individuals. Adjoining this entrance all there is a second, narrower, room —in which consciousness, too, resides. But on the threshold between these two rooms a watchman performs his function. . . . Now I know you will say that these ideas are both crude and fantastic and quite impermissible in a scientific account. I know they are crude: and more than that, I know they are incorrect, and if I am not mistaken, I already have something better to take their place. Whether they will seem to you equally fantastic I cannot tell. They are preliminary working hypotheses. . . . and they are not to be despised in so far as they are of service in making our observations intelligible. I should like to assure you that these crude hypotheses of the two rooms, the watchman at the threshold between them and consciousness as a spectator at the end of the second room, must nevertheless be far-reaching approximations to the real facts.*[96]

In fact, such architectural metaphors and the topology that they sustain are needed precisely because the unconscious can never be directly observed. When defending their use, Freud argues that "it appeared a legitimate course to supplement the theories which were a direct expression of experience by hypotheses which were designed to facilitate the handling of the material and related to matters which could not be a subject of immediate observation."[97] The superstructure covers over this constitutional blindness. Unable to be seen, the psyche can only be projected off the surfaces that confront the analyst. Freudian theory requires an image of depth beyond surface, the image of the psyche as an interior. Architecture provides this image. It is a structural ornament, a supplementary image that can never be abandoned in favor of a basic observation because it is precisely the image for that which cannot be seen. And more than this, it is an image of seeing. In his discussion of the interior space everything turns on the wall's capacity to block sight and the role of the "watchman" guarding the doors of the room in which the conscious resides as a "spectator": "The impulses in the entrance hall of the unconscious are out of sight of the conscious, which is in the other room."[98] The peculiar

Mark Wigley

status of this metaphor, and the whole chain of references to architecture it is part of that is written everywhere into Freud's corpus, despite his attempt to detach it, becomes even more striking when it recalled that Freud claimed in a letter to Wilhelm Fliess dated January 4, 1898 that "I have an infamously low capacity for visualizing spatial relationships."[99] The spatial image called up when the theory cannot see is itself obscure. It covers over a gap in the theory that can neither be effaced or faced.

It is in this sense, then, that architecture, or rather a certain account of architecture, operates as a fetish in Freud's text. If the fetishist's fear of castration "sets up a sort of permanent memorial to itself by creating this substitute,"[100] psychoanalytic theory's anxiety about its own mastery sets up architecture itself as a substitute for that authority even, if not especially, evident in its attempt to master the enigmatic scene of fetishism. But for what, in the end, is architecture a substitute? Which kind of gap does it cover over? Why can't it be discarded? What would its removal expose that is so frightening?

Having discredited the metaphor for a second time in "Constructions in Analysis," for example, Freud insists on the importance of the term *construction* over the term *interpretation*. But what precisely is left of this word after it is disassociated from buildings? Or rather, what was gained by the association with buildings in the first place? The metaphor loses no rhetorical force despite its apparent implausibility. Freud's attempt to restrain the metaphor and its endless return, even within that attempt, suggests that it does not simply "stand for" what it appears to represent, that at some level an ambivalence between decoration and structure is part of the collective associations that the canonic image of architecture invokes, even while being employed to resist precisely such an ambivalence.

After all, psychoanalytic theory's relationship with architecture must, at a certain point, be subjected to psychoanalysis. Freud repeatedly identifies the traditional construction of theory with the way in which "secondary revision" in the dream work (like the delusions of the first theories of the child) "fills in the gaps" to construct a smooth dissimulating facade masking the traumatic observation of particular gaps in the world. Psychoanalysis claims to embrace all such gaps, flaws, errors, and slips in an unstable architecture that is itself congenitally flawed and in which the roles of structure and decorative surface often reverse. But this self-description is itself a facade.

Just as the facade of the dream and the joke can employ irrationality to disguise rationality, the explicit destabilization of the canonic image of architecture found throughout Freud's writing may disguise its claims to high theoretical status, claims that can only be made by preserving that very image.

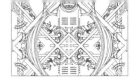

Just as the inherent but repressed instability of high theoretical structures has been identified by post-structuralist readings of the canonic texts, the traditional architectonic pretensions of high theory can be found within the apparently unstable architecture of psychoanalytic texts. In both cases the architectural metaphor is both indispensable and fickle, turning over and over and forever slipping sideways. And more than this, it both stands for and against this very kind of slippage. The classical opposition between stable structure and mobile ornament is, at the very least, doubly unstable.

This rhetorical slippage organizes, for example, Freud's use of the term *construction*, which ostensibly refers to a formation with a particular history, something assembled in a certain way that could have been built differently, but also exploits its associations with the sense of trans-historical immutable order sustained by the image of a building conforming to certain precultural structural principles like gravity. The psyche may be a historical artifact but its different possibilities depend on, and are limited by, certain fundamental structural principles. This strategic ambivalence can be traced throughout contemporary critical discourse where the word *construction* has acquired an extraordinarily important role. Writers like David Harvey covertly exploit this ambiguity while attempting to sustain the traditional institution of theory; but it also organizes discourses that attempt to undermine that institution.

If fetishes only exist in theory, architecture is the theoretical fetish, the fetish of theory. As the traditional paradigm throughout the Western theoretical tradition of ideas embedded in material, it stands for theory.

The fetishism of architecture that makes theory possible complicates any explicit theory of architectural space like that offered by Harvey. It is not that a more rigorous reading of space would have to be psychoanalytic. Rather, it would address the specific images of space upon which the institution of theory covertly depends before that institution overtly "reads" the question of space, let alone particular spaces. This would involve interrogating the "material" practices of theoretical production, including, if not especially, those of psychoanalysis. To take these practices, which cannot be separated from the specific theories they produce, for granted is to remain complicitous with traditional mechanisms of exploitation involved in the production of the spaces that the theories then claim to examine, if not criticize.

Of all of these theoretical practices, perhaps the most exemplary is the rejection of the mask in favor of the interior, the ornament in favor of the structure. But the strange life of architecture within the institutions of theory actually complicates the geometry of the mask, undermining the distinction between an "inside" hidden behind the mask and an "outside" exposed in front

Mark Wigley

of it. The distinction, so necessary to *both* the traditional economies of exploitation and the multiple forms of class, race, gender and sexuality specific forms of resistance to them, is itself an exemplary form of mystification produced by the surfaces that appear to merely mark the division. It only exists within the surface of the mask. It is literally a surface effect.

The possibility of political critique therefore lies on, rather than behind, the surface. Indeed, it requires a certain fetishism of surface. Fetishism becomes a possibility of resistance, as exemplified by much of the feminist work that exploits the structural role of surface in order to subvert the abusive agenda organizing the traditional identification of "woman" with surface, mask and ornament. This is the very work condemned by Harvey in order to define his project, and proclaim its status as a meta-theory of space.

Canonic Freudian psychoanalytic theory does not simply offer a ready-made alternative to this routine power play by making available a less suspect theory of space. Indeed, the same subordination of masquerade and its identification with woman is embedded in Freud's covert pretension to high theory and is entangled with the orthodox use of the architectural metaphor implicated in that pretension. This can be seen, for example, in what is perhaps Freud's very first theoretical use of the image of architecture, which includes his first reference to the idea of "facade." In May 1897 Freud sent Wilhelm Fleiss two drafts of an unpublished manuscript called "The Architecture of Hysteria" that marked, for him, the "consolidation" of his thinking and "a great advance in insight."[101] The drafts describe psychoanalysis as the attempt to read through the successive layers of fantasies "constructed" as "psychic facades" to "make inaccessible" the patient's memories.[102] In this layering of surfaces, which one of his accompanying letters describes as "embellishments" of the "facts," each one is put up by repression, a psychic mechanism that is described as "feminine." "It is to be supposed that the element essentially responsible for repression is always what is feminine."[103]

Freud appears to reject this sexualization of the architecture of the psyche shortly after he renounced the seduction theory, on which the drafts were based, in his infamous letter to Fliess on September 21, 1897. On November 14 he sends another letter which announces that at last he has found "the essential thing lying behind" repression: infantile forms of sexuality which play across the whole surface of the body before being successively abandoned and covered over in stages. Psychic facades are no longer simply the products of hysteria but are the results of "normal repression." The architecture of the psyche is detached from the sexuality "behind" it. After sketching this new position, which would become central to psychoanalysis, Freud claims to "have

also given up the idea of explaining libido as the masculine factor and repression a s the feminine one."[104] But even though he insists on this point in later essays,[105] it is contradicted by much of the rhetoric he employs. Psychoanalysis never completely effaced the traces of its origins in the study of hysteria, which had always been identified with femininity.

It is not just that Freud's theory subordinates woman but that psychoanalysis is itself, by definition, a reading through, a going beyond, of the "feminine" surfaces, the facades erected as psychic defenses. Despite the reversal of the subordinate role of the surface (facade, ornament, supplement, mask, accessory, etc.) found everywhere in Freud's theory, it, in the end, privileges the structure said to be behind the mask. For all its explicit destabilization of the traditional image of architecture, it is unable to confront the possibility raised by Lou Andreas-Salome in one of her first letters to Freud (dated November 9, 1912) that the "secondary" feminine masks that act as "defenses" actually organize the psychic structure that they appear to cover and protect:

> Certainly these are purely feminine means to the unvarying masculine
> end-goal, and only appear independent to the superficial observer. But it
> is a question whether this conception of them as pure means is not equally
> superficial, and whether they are not only masks, but actually masks of
> masks, i.e. whether, although the ego-ideal thinks that it is making use of
> them for symbolic purposes, they are not in fact making use of the ego-ideal
> as image and metaphor, in order to achieve their purpose.[106]

What is being suggested here is that this structural role of the surface can always be found within the exchange of "architecture" as a kind of commodity in the overt and covert economies of both high theory and the so-called practices of everyday life, even where architecture is being appropriated precisely to resist that possibility. The figure of architecture is, like all fetishes, at least double, slipping constantly between exemplifying the subordination of the surface and exemplifying its dominance. It is only in terms of this slippage, which is itself a surface effect, that a political reading of architecture becomes possible and is at once transformed into an architectural reading of politics.

The research for this paper was carried out under a fellowship at the Chicago Institute for Architecture and Urbanism.

Footnotes

1. William Pietz, "The Problem of the Fetish, I," *Res*, no. 9 (1985): 10. Pietz carefully traces the history of the term beginning with "the formation of inhabited intercultural spaces along the Western African Coast"(6).

2. "This method studies the history of the usage of "fetish" as a field of exemplary instances that exemplify no model or truth prior to or outside this very 'archive' itself; it views the fetish as a radically historical object that is nothing other than the totalized series of its particular usages," (ibid., 7).

3. Freud, for example, begins his essay on fetishism: "In the last few years I have had an opportunity of studying analytically a number of men whose object-choice was ruled by a fetish. One need not suppose that these persons had sought analysis on account of a fetish; the devotees of fetishes regard them as abnormalities, it is true, but rarely as symptoms of illness; usually they are quite content with them or even extol the advantages they offer for erotic gratification. As a rule, therefore, the fetish made its appearance in analysis as a secondary finding," (Sigmund Freud, "Fetishism" (1927), *Sexuality and the Psychology of Love*, trans. Joan Riviere (New York: Macmillan, 1963), 212.

4. See Mark Wigley, "The Translation of Architecture: The Production of Babel," *Assemblage*, no. 8 (1989): 7–22.

5. Jean Baudrillard, "Fetishism and Ideology: The Semiological Reduction," *Towards a Political Economy of the Sign*, trans. Charles Levin (St. Louis: Telos) 1981; first published in *Nouvelle Revue de Psychanalyse* 2 (Autumn 1970), 89.

6. Fredric Jameson, "Postmodernism or the Cultural Logic of Late Capitalism," *New Left Review*, no. 146 (1984): 53–92.

7. David Harvey, *The Condition of Postmodernity* (Oxford: Basil Blackwood, 1989).

8. Edward Soja, *Postmodern Geographies: The Reassertion of Space in Critical Social Theory* (London: Verso, 1989).

9. Harvey, *The Condition of Postmodernity*, 58.

10. Ibid., 88. "There has emerged an attachment to surfaces rather than to roots, to collage rather than in-depth work, to superimposed quoted images rather than worked surfaces, to a collapsed sense of time and space rather than solidly achieved cultural artefact" (61).

11. Ibid., 66.

12. Ibid., 58. Harvey cites Jameson's claim that "the world thereby momentarily loses its depth and threatens to become a glossy skin, a stereoscopic illusion, a rush of filmic images without density" (54). In fact, Harvey's whole argument is indebted to Jameson's essay, which identifies the fetishism ("both in the Freudian and in the Marxian sense") of Andy Warhol's "postmodern" art with the way in which its "decorative exhilaration" privileges surface: "the emergence of a new kind of flatness or depthlessness, a new kind of superficiality in the most literal sense—perhaps the supreme formal feature of all the postmodernisms"(Jameson, "Postmodernism," 60) but uses architecture as the paradigm: "architecture is, however, of all the arts that closest constitutively to the economic, with which, in the form of commissions and land values, it has virtually unmediated relationship" (56); "Architecture therefore remains in this sense the privileged aesthetic language; and the distorting and fragmenting reflection of one enormous glass surface to the other can be taken as paradigmatic of the central role of process and reproduction in postmodern culture" (79). In postmodern space, as in postmodern theory, "depth is replaced by surface, or by multiple surfaces. . . . Nor is this depthlessness merely metaphorical . . . this strange new surface in its own preemptory way renders our older systems of perception of the city somehow archaic and aimless, without offering another in their place" (62).

13. Ibid., 87.

14. Ibid., 53. With the postmodern concern with "surface appearances rather than roots," "the search for roots ends up at worst being produced and marketed as an image" (303).

15. Ibid., 100.

16. Ibid., 77.

17. Ibid., 100.

18. In Marx's key chapter on fetishism—" The Fetishism of the Commodity and its Secret"—for example, it is not surprising to find the reassertion of the earlier foundation/superstructure argument (Karl Marx, *Capital: A Critique of Political Economy*, trans. Ben Fowkes [New York: Vintage, 1977], 1:175).

19. Karl Marx, "Results of the Immediate Process of Production," *Capital* 1:10003 (appendix).

20. Harvey, *The Condition of Postmodernity*, 165.

21. Ibid., 167.

22. "It is this that forms the foundation for the fetishism of the political economists" (Marx,*Capital* 1:983). Fetishism "consists in regarding *economic* categories, such as being in *commodity*, or

productive labor, as qualities inherent in the material incarnations of these formal determinations or categories." (1046)

23. Postmodernism is "actually celebrating the activity of masking and cover-up, all the fetishisms of locality, place, or social grouping, while denying that kind of meta-theory which can grasp the political-economic processes . . . that are becoming ever more universalizing in their depth, intensity, reach and power over everyday life" (Harvey, *The Condition of Postmodernity*, 117).

24. Ibid., 101.

25. "The historical and anthropological record is full of examples of how varied the concepts of space can be, while investigations of the spatial worlds of children, the mentally ill (particularly schizophrenics), oppressed minorities, women and men of different class, rural and urban dwellers, etc., illustrate a similar diversity within outwardly homogeneous populations. Yet some sense of an overarching and objective meaning of space which we must, in the last instance, all acknowledge is pervasive.

    I think it is important to challenge the idea of a single and objective sense of time and space, against which we can measure the diversity of human conceptions and perceptions" (ibid., 203). But these different spatialities are not examined by the text which immediately goes on to argue that we "properly ground" all concepts of space in "material processes." The point is that this image of grounding in material is itself a particular concept of space, an ideological formation available for critique, and that it is precisely its exemption from critique that makes possible the dominant rhetoric of theoretical production—theory as well-constructed, solid argument that goes behind facades to identify the solid structure of phenomena. Harvey denies an "overarching meaning of space" in order to produce his own overarching theory of space.

26. Ibid., 117. The words are Terry Eagleton's, approvingly cited by Harvey. Eagleton returns the endorsement on the back cover of the book by describing it in the totalizing terms of the traditional metaphor of theory cutting through the ephemeral surface to the structural base: "Devastating. The most brilliant theoretical debates about postmodernity to date. David Harvey cuts beneath the theoretical debates about postmodernist culture to reveal the social and economic basis of this apparently free-floating phenomenon. After reading this book, those who fashionably scorn the idea of a total critique had better think again."

27. Ibid., 91.

28. Ibid., 57.

29. Ibid., 102.

30. Ibid., 7.

31. Ibid., 101.

32. Marx, *Capital*, 1:176.

33. Harvey, *The Condition of Postmodernity*, 50.

34. Ibid., 64.

35. Rosalyn Deutsche, "Men in Space," *Strategies*, no. 3. (1990): 135.

36. "By referring all the problems of 'fetishism' back to superstructural mechanisms of false consciousness, Marxism eliminates any real chance it has of analyzing the *actual process of ideological labor*. By refusing to analyze the structures and the mode of ideological production inherent in its own logic, Marxism is condemned (behind the facade of 'dialectical' discourse in terms of class struggle) to expanding the reproduction of ideology, and thus of the capitalist system itself. Thus the problem of the generalized 'fetishization' of real life forces us to reconsider the problem of the reproduction of ideology. The *fetishistic* theory of infrastructure and superstructure must be exploded, and replaced by a more comprehensive theory of productive forces, since these are *all structurally* implicated in the capitalist system—and not only in some cases (i.e. material production), while merely superstructurally in others (i.e. ideological production)" (Baudrillard, "Fetishism and Ideology," 89).

37. See Mark Wigley, "Architecture after Philosophy: Le Corbusier and the Emperor's New Paint," *Journal of the Philosophy of the Visual Arts* 2 (1990): 84–89.

38. "There is a cancer of the object: this proliferation of astructural elements which makes for the triumphalism of the object is a sort of cancer. Now it is on these astructural elements, (automatism, accessories, inessential differences) that the entire circuit of fashion and of directed consumption is organized" (*Systeme des objets* [Paris: Gallimard, 1968], cited in Naomi Schor, *Reading in Detail: Aesthetics of the Feminine* [New York: Routledge, 1987], 56).

39. For example, see Jean Baudrillard, *Seduction*, trans., Brian Singer (New York: St. Martin's, 1990; French edition, 1979). For a critique of this later Baudrillard, see Meaghan Morris, "Room 101 Or A Few Worst Things in the World," *The Pirate's Fiancé: Feminism, Reading, Postmodernism* (New York: Verso, 1988).

40. Baudrillard, "Fetishism and Ideology," 90.

41. Pietz, "The Problem of the Fetish," 10.

42. Freud, "a fetish is constructed . . . with the help of displacement." Sigmund Freud, *An Outline of Psycho-Analysis* (1940), trans. James Strachey (New York: Norton, 1969), 60.

43. Freud, "Fetishism," *Sexuality and the Psychology of Love*, 219.

44. Freud, "Constructions in Analysis" (1937), *Standard Edition*, trans. James Strachey (London: Hogarth, 1959), 20:259.

45. Ibid., 260.

46. Ibid.

47. "For we learn from it that no damage is done if, for once in a way, we make a mistake and offer a wrong construction as the probable truth. . . . Some suitable opportunity . . . will arise when some new material has come to light which allows us to make a better construction and so to correct our error. In this way the false construction drops out, as if it had never been made; and, indeed, we often get an impression as though, to borrow from the words of Polonius, our bait of falsehood had taken a carp of truth . . . new memories which complete and extend the construction" (ibid., 261). Likewise, Freud describes the structural role of the flaws in the child's first theories about sexuality that permanently organize the psyche: "These false sexual theories. . . . each one of them, contain a bit of the real truth" (Sigmund Freud, "On the Sexual Theories of Children" [1908], *Standard Edition*).

48. Freud, *An Outline of Psychoanalysis*, 52–53.

49. Samuel Weber, "The Divaricator: Remarks on Freud's *Witz*," *Glyph*, no. 1 (1977): 1–27.

50. Philosophy is always "clinging to the illusion of being able to present a picture of the universe which is without gaps and is coherent . . . [The philosopher] patches up the gaps in the structure of the universe" (Sigmund Freud, *New Introductory Lectures on Psychoanalysis* [1933], trans. James Strachey [New York: Norton, 1965], 160).

51. "A speculative theory of the relations in question would begin by seeking to *construct* a clearly delineated concept as its *foundation*. In my opinion, however, that is precisely the difference between a speculative theory and a science *erected upon* the interpretation of empirical data. The latter will not envy speculation its privilege of having a *smooth, logically unassailable foundation*, but will gladly settle for the nebulous, evanescent, scarcely imaginable basic thoughts, which it hopes to grasp more clearly in the course of its development, or which it is even prepared to exchange for others. For these ideas are not the *foundations of science, upon which everything rests*: that, on the contrary is the observation alone. *They are not the foundation-stone, but the top of the whole structure*, and they can be replaced and discarded without damaging it" Sigmund Freud, "On Narcissism: An Introduction" (1914), *Standard Edition* 14:77 [my italics]).

52. Freud, *An Outline of Psychoanalysis*, 53.

53. Freud, "On the Sexual Theories of Children," *Standard Edition*, vol. 9.

54. Freud, "Constructions in Analysis," *Standard Edition* 20:268.

55. Ibid., 268.

56. Freud, *An Outline of Psychoanalysis*, 60.

57. Freud, "Fetishism," *Sexuality and the Psychology of Love*, 216.

58. "Thus there is a conflict between the demand of the instinct and the prohibition of reality. But in fact the child takes neither course, or rather he takes both simultaneously, which comes to the same thing. He replies to the conflict with two contrary reactions, both of which are valid and effective. On the one hand, with the help of certain mechanisms he rejects reality and refuses to except any prohibition; on the other hand, in the same breath he recognizes the danger of reality, takes over the fear of that danger as a pathological symptom and tries subsequently to divest himself of that fear" Sigmund Freud, " Splitting of the Ego in the Process of Defence," *Standard Edition* 20: 275.

59. Freud, "Fetishism," *Sexuality and the Psychology of Love*, 214.

60. Alan Bass, "On the History of a Mistranslation and the Psychoanalytic Movement" in Joseph F. Graham, ed. *Difference in Translation* (Ithaca, NY: Cornell University Press, 1985).

61. Sigmund Freud, *Leonardo da Vinci and a Memory of His Childhood* (1910), trans. Alan Tyson. (New York: Norton, 1961).

62. Ibid., 112–113.

63. "Infantile sexual researches begin very early, sometimes before the third year of life. They do not relate to the distinction between the sexes, for this means nothing to the children, since they (or at any rate boys) attribute the same male genital to both sexes. If, afterwards, a boy makes the discovery of the vagina from seeing his little sister or a girl playmate, he tries, to begin with, to disavow the evidence of his senses, for he cannot imagine a human creature like himself who is without such a precious portion. Later on, he takes fright at the possibility thus presented to him; any threats that may have been made to him earlier, because he took too intense an interest in his little organ, now produce a deferred effect. He comes under the sway of the castration complex, the form taken by which plays a great part in the construction of his character." (Sigmund Freud, *Introductory Lectures on Psychoanalysis* (1917) trans. James Strachey [New York: Norton, 1966], 318).

64. Bass, "*On the History of Mistranslation*," 111.

65. Freud, "Fetishism," *Sexuality and the Psychology of Love*, 217.

66. Sigmund Freud, "An Autobiographical Study," (1935), *Standard Edition* 20:72.

67. Freud, "Fetishism," *Sexuality and the Psychology of Love*, 217.

68. Ibid., 215.

69. Freud, *An Outline of Psychoanalysis*, 61.

70. Freud, "Splitting the Ego in the Process of Defence," *Standard Edition* 20:275.

71. "From the point of view of classification, we should no doubt have done better to have mentioned this highly interesting group of aberrations of the sexual instinct among the deviations in respect of the sexual *object*. But we have postponed their mention till . . . " (Sigmund Freud, *Three Essays on the Theory of Sexuality*, trans. James Strachey, [London: Imago, 1949], 31).

72. Jacques Lacan and Wladimir Granoff, "Fetishism: The Symbolic, the Imaginary and the Real" in Sandor Lorand, ed., *Perversions: Psychodynamics and Therapy* (New York: Grammercy, 1956), 265; Karl Abraham, "Remarks on the Psychoanalysis of a Case of Foot and Corset Fetishism" (1911), *Selected Papers of Karl Abraham*, trans. Douglas Bryan and Alix Strachey (New York: Basic Books, 1953), 125.

73. Sigmund Freud, "On the Genesis of Fetishism," ed. and trans. Louis Rose, in Freud and Fetishism: Previously Unpublished Minutes of the Vienna Psychoanalytic Society," *Psychoanalytic Quarterly* 57 (1988): 150.

74. Ibid., 148.

75. *The Freud/Jung Letters*, ed. William McGuire, trans. Ralph Manheim and R.F.C. Hull. (Princeton: Princeton University Press, 1974), 265, cited in "On the History of a Mistranslation and the Psychoanalytic Movement," 112.

76. Freud, *Three Essays on the Theory of Sexuality*, 34.

77. Freud, "An Autobiographical Study," *Standard Edition* 20:70.

78. Freud, *Three Essays on the Theory of Sexuality*, 32.

79. "No other variation on the sexual instinct that borders upon the pathological can lay so much claim as this one, such is the peculiarity of the phenomena to which it gives rise" (ibid., 32.).

80. Freud, *An Outline of Psychoanalysis*, 22.

81. Freud, *Three Essays on the Theory of Sexuality*, 50.

82. Ibid.

83. Freud, "On the Genesis of Fetishism," 151. Richard von Krafft Ebing was the professor of psychiatry at the University of Vienna whose *Psychopathia Sexualis* (1886) introduced the term *fetishism* as part of the first systematic account of sexual pathologies.

84. "Children may thus be described as 'polymorphously perverse,' and if these impulses only show traces of activity, that is because on the one hand they are of less intensity compared with those in later life and on the other hand all of a child's sexual manifestations are at once energetically suppressed by education. This suppression is, as it were, extended into theory; for adults endeavor to overlook one portion of the sexual manifestations of children and to disguise another portion by misinterpreting its sexual nature, so that they can disavow the whole of them" (Freud, *Introductory Lectures on Psychoanalysis*, 209).

85. Jaqueline Rose, *Sexuality in the Field of Vision* (London: Verso, 1986), 196.

86. Freud, *Introductory Lectures on Psychoanalysis*, 349.

87. Freud, *New Introductory Lectures on Psychoanalysis*, 21.

88. Freud, *Introductory Lectures on Psychoanalysis*, 181.

89. Sigmund Freud, *The Interpretation of Dreams* (1900), trans. James Strachey (New York: Avon, 1965), 245.

90. Symptomatically, Freud maintains the facade of the very dream he uses as an exemplar. It is precisely here, in discussing a dream in which the unconscious material has forced its way through to the surface and less work of translation is needed because the facade is less secure, that Freud withholds his own interpretation of his own dream: "I must also refrain from any detailed analysis of the two remaining episodes of the dream. . . . It will rightly be suspected that what compels me to make this suppression is sexual material; but there is no need to rest content with this explanation. After all, there are many things which one has to keep secret from other people but of which one makes no secret to oneself" (ibid., 245). The material doesn't break through the surface of the text. Even though the memory of the dream is published, its construction remains masked. For detailed analyses of the dream, the second most influential dream in the book and the one that produces the most information about Freud's infantile sexuality, see Didier Anzien, *Freud's Self-Analysis*, trans. Peter Graham (Madison: International Universities Press, 1986), 336–351, and Alexander Grinstein, *On Sigmund Freud's Dreams* (Detroit, MI: Wayne State University Press, 1968), 92–160.

91. Freud, *Introductory Lectures on Psychoanalysis*, 291.

92. Sigmund Freud, "Jokes and their Relation to the Unconscious" (1905), *Standard Edition* 8:108.

93. Ibid., 105.

94. In a late supplement to *The Interpretation of Dreams* Freud notes that "we know now that the manifest content is an illusion, *a facade*. It is not worthwhile to submit it to an ethical examination or to take its breaches of morality any more seriously than its breaches of logic or mathematics." (Sigmund Freud, "Some Additional Notes on Dream-Interpretation as a Whole," *Therapy and Technique* [New York: Macmillan, 1963], 223. But, noting that the existence of such an "immoral facade" still raises the question of why the sophisticated and endlessly ingenuitive censorship mechanisms do not always produce a moral facade, he argues that "some of them are innocent boastings or identifications that put up a mask of pretence; they have not been censored because they do not tell the truth. But others of them and it must be admitted, the majority, really mean what they say and have undergone no distortion. They are the expression of immoral, incestuous and perverse impulses of murderous or sadistic lusts . . . . The censorship has neglected its task, this has been noticed too late, and the development of anxiety is a substitute for the distortion that has been omitted. . . . But our interest in these *manifestly* immoral dreams is greatly reduced when we find from analysis that the majority of dreams, innocent dreams . . . are the fulfillments of immoral—egoistic, sadistic, perverse or incestuous—wishful impulses. As in the world of the waking life, these masked criminals are far commoner than those with their visors raised" (ibid., 224).

95. "The subdivision of the unconscious is a part of an attempt to picture the apparatus of the mind as being built up of a number of *functional systems* whose interrelations may be expressed in spatial terms, without reference, of course, to the actual brain. (I have described this as the *topographical* method of approach.) Such ideas as these are part of a speculative superstructure of psychoanalysis, any portion of which can be abandoned or damaged without loss or regret the moment its inadequacy has been proved" (Freud, "An Autobiographical Study," *Standard Edition* 20:59).

96. Freud, *Introductory Lectures on Psychoanalysis*, 295.

97. Freud, "An Autobiographical Study," *Standard Edition* 20: 59

98. Freud, *Introductory Lectures on Psychoanalysis*, 295.

99. *The Complete Letters of Sigmund Freud to Wilhelm Fleiss: 1887–1904.* ed. and trans. Jeffrey Masson (Cambridge, MA: Harvard University, 1985), 292.

100. Freud, "Fetishism," *Sexuality and the Psychology of Love*, 216.

101. Masson, *The Complete Letters*, 239.

102. "For fantasies are psychic facades produced in order to bar access to these memories" (Freud, Draft L, "The Architecture of Hysteria," May 2, 1987, *Complete Letters*, 240.

103. The second draft sent to Fleiss on May 25, 1897, begins: "Probably like this: some of the scenes are accessible directly, but others are arranged in order of increasing resistance; the more slightly repressed ones come [to light] first, but only incompletely on account of their association with the severely repressed ones. The path taken by [analytic] work first goes down in loops to the scenes or to their proximity, then from a symptom a little deeper down, and then again from a symptom deeper still. Since most of the scenes are combined in the few symptoms, our path makes repeated loops through the background thoughts of the same symptoms, It is to be supposed that the element essentially responsible for repression is always that which is feminine" (Freud, Draft M, "The Architecture of Hysteria," ibid., 246.

104. Ibid., 281.

105. "The theory of psycho-analysis (a theory based on observation) holds firmly to the view that the motive force of repression must not be sexualized." Sigmund Freud, "A Child is Being Beaten" (1919), *Sexuality and the Psychology of Love*, 132.

106. Ernst Pfeiffer, *Sigmund Freud and Lou Andreas-Salome: Letters*, trans. William and Elaine Robson-Scott (London: Hogarth, 1972), 9.

Illustrations

1. Ashanti fetish house.
2. Ashanti fetish doctor.
3. From David Harvey, *The Condition of Postmodernity* (Oxford: Basil Blackwell Ltd., 1989). Gallery at Harbor Place, Baltimore, Maryland. Photograph by David Harvey.
4. Manhattan fetish doctors at the Manhattan architect's costume ball. Left to right: A. Stewart Walker as the Fuller building, Leonard Schultze as the Waldorf-Astoria, Ely Jacques Kahn as the Squibb Building, William Van Alen as the Chrysler Building, Ralph Walker as No. 1 Wall Street, D. E. Ward as the Metropolitan Tower, and J. H. Freedlander as the Museum of the City of New York.
5. From *The Condition of Postmodernity*. Cover with *Dream of Liberty*, 1974, by Madelon Vriesendorp. Deutsches Architekturmuseum, Frankfurt am Main.
6. Ibid. David Salle, '*Tight as Houses*'. Galerie Bruno Bischofberger, Zurich.
7. Ibid. Titian, *The Venus d'Urbino*. Mansell Collection.

8.   Ibid. Edouard Manet, *Olympia.* Musée d'Orsay, Cliché des Musées Nationaux, Paris.

9.   Ibid. Robert Rauschenberg, *Persimmon.* Leo Castelli Gallery, New York, © Robert Rauschenberg. © DACS 1988 (photograph by Rudolph Burckhardt).

10.   Ibid. Advertisement for Citizen Watches. Lintas Limited, London.

11.   Ibid. Charles Moore, Piazza d'Italia, New Orleans. Deutsches Architekturmuseum, Frankfurt am Main.

12.   Ibid.Scarlett Place of Baltimore

13.   Margin notes by Sigmund Freud from the manuscript draft of "Fetishism."

14.   Drawing by Sigmund Freud of analytic encounter with facades from his manuscript of "The Architecture of Hysteria."

ANN BERGREN

MOUSEION

MUSE I AM

M
e

M
o
r
y

M

t
heFetish

Murals
Buildings

V
e
n
i
c   e,   ca   n
                                    a
                      building   remember

m
o
u
s
e
î
o
n

haunt and shrine of the Muses

museum

The house was, besides, a repository of centuries of **memory** and tradition, **embodied in its walls** and objects: the walls were marked by crumbling stones and the "discoloration of ages"; . . . it was, in fact, **already a museum**, a collection . . . here preserved in the memory of the family.

Then the contrast between the walled-up windows on the ground floor and the empty windows on the upper floor, "opening onto the shadows of the interior," gave a **quasi-anthropomorphic** air to the structure.

A. Vidler, *Assemblage* 3 (1987): 8.

The TEXTS and Textures of Urban   Memory
SciARC march1987

    can an   ***urbs***   remember?
    a "dumb object" be a   TEXT
                    "screen memory"
                    fetish
                    [*folie*, folly]?
                pseudea homoia etumoisin

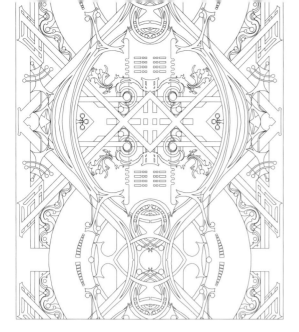

At once a **psychological** and an **aesthetic** phenomenon, it simultaneously **established** and **destabilized.** Its effects were guaranteed by an original authenticity, a first burial, and made all the more potent by virtue of **a return** that, in civilization, was **in a real sense out of place.** Something was not, then, merely **haunted**, but rather **revisited by a power** that was **thought dead.**

A. Vidler, Assemblage 3 (1987): 12.

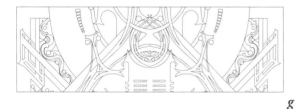

g

host stories to make you feel at home

SMOKE

Sixty acres, 14 miles west of Los Angeles, overlooking the Pacific Ocean just south of Santa Monica. Bought by Abbot Kinney in 1904.

A century earlier, Indians from the offshore islands visited the area to collect decorative marine shells.

Formerly part of La Ballone Rancho, a land grant deeded to the Machado and Talamantes families by the Mexican government in 1839.

132

1. Abbot Kinney, *Founder of 'Venice-of-America'*

2. Arches of St. Mark's, Venice, Ca.

Born 1850 to influential New Jersey family. Educated in France, Switzerland, Heidelberg.

Suffered from insomnia. Travelled around the world to find a climate to "end his sleepless nights." At Sierra Madre Inn, fell asleep on billiard table for "the best damn night's sleep" he ever had.

Built citrus ranch nearby named "Kinneloa," a contraction of his name and the Kanaka word for hillside.

A Democrat and follower of William Jennings Bryan. With Helen Hunt Jackson (author of *Ramona*) made a government-sponsored study of Ca. Mission Indians and recommended reforms.

Won coin flip with co-owners of oceanfront property—beautiful on the north, marshy on the south. "I'll take the marshes," he said. "You'd a gotten the marshes if we'd won," his ex-partners jeered. "*Not if you see what I see,*" he replied.

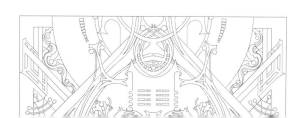

Here, we are reminded of a similar pattern of **uncanny repetition** in Freud's description of his strange experience of a particular quarter in a provincial town, "the character of which could not long remain in doubt," as **painted women filled the windows** of the small houses.

A. Vidler, *Assemblage* 3 (1987): 15.

3. Polyhymnia, one of the nine Muses of ancient Greece

134

4. Venus of "Venice on the Half-Shell" mural

TEXT — *textum* 'WOVEN object'

mêtis — the working and the work of 'transformative intelligence'

Metis — goddess swallowed pregnant by Zeus mother of Athena

Athena — warrior goddess
teaches WEAVING to women

    Looking backward toward Boticelli and the Classical tradition of "modest Venus" types he remembered, and forward toward the graffiti of Venice, Ca. written upon her.

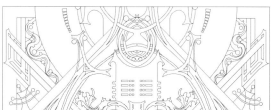

Woman's weaving—her text—is a signal instance of the inebriated oscillation of truth and imitation, stability and mobility, sound and silence, speech and writing, and writing and drawing that constitutes for Greek the *graphé*—an ambiguity obscured in languages that attempt a clean break between the graphic and the linguistic, between building as "dumb object" and language: for example, English 'draw' vs. 'write' (though 'draw' means 'write' in "draw a contract"), French *dessiner* vs. *écrire*, German *zeichnen* vs. *schreiben*, Italian *disegnare* vs. *scrivere*.

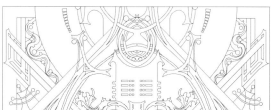

The myth of Tereus, Procne, and Philomela is an eloquent example. When Tereus, husband of Procne, rapes her sister Philomela, he cuts out the woman's tongue to keep her silent—to keep her from telling her sister, his wife. Philomela responds with a *mêtis* that imitates her castrated voice. She "wove *grammata* in a robe" which she sent to her sister—*grammata* indecidably 'pictures/writing' (*gramma* and *graphé* are cognate: *graph-* + *ma* > *gramma*). In her power to express what she knows through the silence of dumb material, the female is the mistress of the graphic, of the constructed *mêtis*.

So prevalent and definitive is the association of weaving and the female that Freud calls it the one contribution of women to civilization and an imitation, in fact, of their own anatomical destiny—the woven threads emulating the pubic veil over her lack of the penis (Freud, "Femininity," SE 22, 132):

> The effect of penis-envy has a share, further, in the physical vanity of women, since they are bound to value their charms more highly as a late compensation for their original sexual inferiority. Shame, which is considered to be feminine characteristic *par excellence* but is far more a matter of convention that might be supposed, has as its purpose, we believe, concealment [*verdecken*: **Decke**, 'cover, ceiling, roof, skin, envelope, coat, pretence, screen'] of genital deficiency. We are not forgetting that at a later time shame takes on other functions. It seems that women have made few contributions to the discoveries and inventions in the history of civilization; there is, however, one technique which they may have invented—that of plaiting and weaving. If that is so, we should be tempted to guess the unconscious motive for the achievement. Nature herself would seem to have given the model which this achievement imitates by causing the growth at maturity of the pubic hair that conceals the genitals. The step that remained to be taken lay in making the threads adhere to one another, while on the body they stick into the skin and are only matted together. If you reject this idea as fantastic and regard my belief in the influence of a lack of a penis on the configuration of femininity as an *idée fixe,* I am of course defenseless.

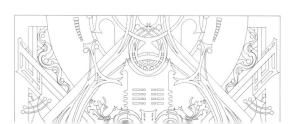

With Freud's account of weaving the female's substitute-penis, compare Gottfried Semper's theory of weaving as the origin of architecture as vertical space enclosure ("The Textile Art." pp. 254–255 and "Structural Elements of Assyrian-Chaldean Architecture." pp. 205–206 in *Gottfried Semper: In Search of Architecture*).

> *. . . the beginning of building coincides with the beginning of textiles. . . .* The wall is that architectural element that formally represents and makes visible *the enclosed space as such*, absolutely, as it were, without reference to secondary concepts.
>
> We might recognize the *pen*, bound together from sticks and branches, and the interwoven *fence* as the earliest vertical spatial enclosure that man *invented. . . .* Weaving the fence led to weaving movable walls. . . . Using wickerwork for setting apart one's property and for floor mats and protection against heat and cold far preceded making even the roughest masonry. Wickerwork was the original motif of the wall. It retained this primary significance, actually or ideally, when the light hurdles and mattings were later transformed into brick or stone walls. The essence of the wall was wickerwork.
>
> In all Germanic languages the word *Wand* ['wall'] (of the same root and same basic meaning as *Gewand* ['garment']) directly recalls the old origin and type of *visible* spatial enclosure. Likewise, **Decke**, *Bekleidung, Schranke, Zaun* (similar to *Saum*), and many other technical expressions are not somewhat late linguistic symbols applied to the building trade, but reliable indications of the textile origin of these building parts.

With a stroke of irony, Freud hits upon a certain truth in the aetiology of architecture: the lack—of shelter, protection, beauty, meaning, value—it attempts to supplement.

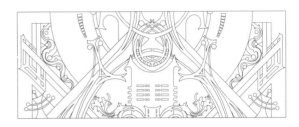

In naming architecture's lack, the female lack of a penis, Freud
> **praises**
(against the will of his text which would downplay the woman's construction)
>   **the** WOVEN **object**
> as a female **Decke**
> 'cover, ceiling, roof,
> skin, envelope, coat,
> pretence, screen'
(imitated by the male architect, whose building of a **Decke** would amount to a substitute—penis envy)
>   **and**
>   **the** TEXT
> as a **Deckerinnerung**
> 'screen memory' and
>   a fetish
(substitute-penis).

fetish

screen memory

Something else has ***taken its place***, has been appointed its ***substitute***, as it were, and now inherits the interest which was formerly directed to its predecessor. But this interest suffers an extraordinary increase as well, because the ***horror of castration has set up a memorial to itself*** in the creation of this substitute.

Freud, *SE 21*, 154.

substitutive formation (Ersatzbildung)

Freud, *SE 6*, 45.

repression accompanied by **replacement** by something in the **neighbourhood** (whether in **space or time**)

Freud, *SE 6*, 52.

It seems rather that when the fetish is instituted some process occurs which reminds one of ***the stopping of memory*** in traumatic amnesia. As in this latter case, the subject's interest comes to a ***halt half-way***, as it were; it is as though ***the last impression before the uncanny and traumatic one*** is ***retained as a fetish***.

instead of the **memory** which would have been justified by the original event, **another memory** is produced which has been to some degree associatively **displaced** from the former one.

Freud, *SE 6*, 52.

. . . fur and velvet—as has long been suspected—are a ***fixation*** of the ***sight of the pubic hair***, which should have been followed by the longed-for sight of the female member.

Freud, *SE 21*, 155.

a case of **displacement** on to something associated **by contiguity**

Freud, *SE 6*, 52.

In very subtle instances ***both the disavowal and the affirmation*** of the castration have found their way into the ***construction*** of the fetish itself. This was so in the case of a man whose fetish was an atheletic support-belt which could also be worn as bathing drawers. This piece of clothing ***covered up*** the genitals entirely and ***concealed the distinction*** between them. Analysis showed that it signified that women were castrated and that they were not castrated; and it also allowed of the hypothesis that men were castrated, for all the possibilities could equally well be ***concealed*** under the belt.

A recollection of this kind, whose value lies in the fact that it represents in the memory impressions and thoughts of a later date whose subject-matter is connected with its own by symbolic or similar links, may appropriately be called a **"screen memory"** [*Deckerinnerung: Decke* **'cover, ceiling, roof, skin, envelope, coat, pretence, pretext, screen'**]

Freud, *SE 6*, 66.

fetish

Affection and hostility in the treatment of the fetish—which run parallel with the disavowal and acknowledgement of castration—are mixed in unequal proportions in different cases, so that the one or the other is more clearly recognizable. We seem here to approach an understanding, even if a distant one, of the behavior of the *'coupeur de nattes.'* [note: A pervert who enjoys **cutting off the hair of the females**.] In him the need to carry out the castration which he disavows has come to the front. His action contains in itself the two mutually incompatible assertions: 'the woman has still got a penis' and 'my father has castrated the woman.'

Freud, *SE 7*, 156

. . . a **first meeting** with the fetish at which it **already aroused sexual interest**. . . . The true explanation is that behind the first recollection of the fetish's appearance there lies a submerged and forgotten phase of sexual development. The **fetish**, like a **"screen memory,"** represents this phase and is thus a remnant and precipitate of it.

Freud, *SE 7*, 154.

screen memory

what provides the intermediate step between a **screen memory** and what it conceals is likely to be a verbal expression.

Freud, *SE 6*, 66.

you know now easily your **intelligence** can **build connecting bridges** from any one point to any other.

Freud, *SE 6*, 65.

"verbal bridges" *(Wortbrücken)*

Freud, *SE 6, 49*

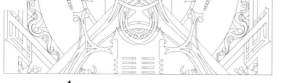

Ann Bergren

mouseîon   *museum*

haunt   of the **Muses**   daughters of Memory and Zeus

The Greek *mouseîon* became the "museum" because all the arts were held to be products of the "speech of the Muses." What do the Muses say?

The **Muses** figure the relation between **memory** and **truth**. In Homer's *Iliad*, before a long catalogue of the Greek ships that will tax his memory, the poet invokes the Muses (Book 2, lines 484–923):

> Speak now to me, Muses, you who live on Olympus, for you are goddesses, you are present beside, and you know all things, but we hear only the report and know nothing. Who were the Danaan leaders and chiefs? The multitude I could not tell or name, not if I had ten tongues, ten mouths, an unbreakable voice, a bronze heart within me, unless the Olympian Muses, daughters of aegis-bearing Zeus, remembered how many came under Ilion.

Because they are "present beside all things" the Muses "have seen" and thus "know" (in Greek, the verb "to know" is "to have seen") everything that their father Zeus rules. By virtue of their mother Memory, they can remember and report to male poets their transcendent knowledge. **Via memory** the Muses are **architects** of *alethea* **"truth"**: speech that **replaces** in the present the totality of the **past place** they have **seen.**

Because of their transcendent knowledge of the truth, the Muses can imitate it perfectly. Handing the staff of poetic inspiration over to the poet Hesiod, the Muses say (*Theogony* lines 27–28):

> We know how to say many false things (*pseudea*) like (*homoia*) to real things (*etumoisin*), and we know, whenever we wish, how to say truth things (*alethea*).

The Muses know how to put *pseudea* "false things' that are **homoia** "same, like, equal" **etumoisin** "to real things" **in the place of truth.** For their past visions they can **substitute** a perfect **Decke,** a perfect **"screen."**

And since the Muses say they can tell the truth, **"whenever we want to,"** who can decide if even this instance of their speech is true? Is this speech one of the *alethea* "truths" or their *pseudea homoia etumoisin* "false things like to real things?" Only one who knows **what the Muses want**?

Was will das Weib? asks Freud in his essay on femininity. "What does the woman want?" The woman covers what she wants. **In that place** she **weaves** her **pubic hair** like an athletic belt.

Vielleicht ist die Wahrheit ein Weib? "Is truth perhaps a woman?" asks Nietzsche in his Preface to the *Gay Science*. "Is her name, to speak Greek, Baubo?" **Baubo** lifted her skirts and **exposed her genitals** to make the mourning Demeter laugh.

To lift her skirt, to analyze the "screen memory" and demystify the fetish, to return the truth that resides in the place of *pseudea homoia etumoisin*, **exposes** not the presence of an erect solid object, but the *alethea* of lack.

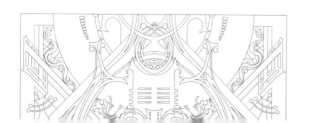

what I see."

V

e

n   C A.

i

c   e,

"Not if you see

The discourse of the fetish . . . began with the formation of inhabited intercultural spaces along the West African coast whose function was to **translate** and **transvalue objects** between radically different social systems.

W. Pietz, *Res* 9 (1985): 6.

The fetish must be viewed as proper to no historical field other than that of the history of the word itself, and to no discrete society or culture, but to a **cross-cultural situation** formed by the **ongoing encounter** of the value codes of **radically different social orders**. In Marxist terms, one might say that the fetish is situated in the **space of cultural revolution**, as the **place** where **the truth of the object as fetish** is **revealed**.

W. Pietz, *Res* 9 (1985): 10–11.

The fetish has an ordering power derived from its status as the fixation or inscription of a **unique originating event** that has brought together **previously heterogeneous** elements into a **novel identity**.

W. Pietz, *Res* 9 (1985): 7.

When he tried to formulate an aesthetic explanation for African fetish worship in 1764, Kant decided that such practices were founded on the principle of the **"trifling"** (*läppish*), the ultimate degeneration of the principle of the beautiful because it lacked all sense of the sublime.

W. Pietz, *Res* 9 (1985): 9.

North Americ *a* Pacific Rim Europe S outh Ameri

Indians

ca

Spaniards

Easterners

Midwesterners

Elderly Jews

Chicanos

Blacks

Beats

Hippies

Drug Addicts

Artists

Sculptors

Architects

Writers

Yuppies

Skaters

Bodybuilders

Movie Producers

Restauranteurs

**MARSHland and
unstable dunes**

Kinney's architect: Norman MARSH

5. Venice Post Office Mural of 1941

Venice Post Office Mural of 1941

screen-remembering the history of Venice   Mnemosyne and Zeus returned.

Present, Muse-like, at the origin, the mural remembers Kinney remembering via the perspectival conventions of Italian Renaissance painting. Vanishing through the point at the top of his head, memory brings back Venice (complete with Ghetto and Bridge of Sighs) and its Classical past in a canal that displaces its source. The mnemonic flow disgorges a triumphal arch, supported by Corinthian columns, over Kinney's wide open eyes, "seeing what I see"

By the working of "substitutive formation," Kinney wears the sign on the door below. It labels him (where his "athletic belt" would be) a master of the *post*, able there to deliver the lack behind the screen.

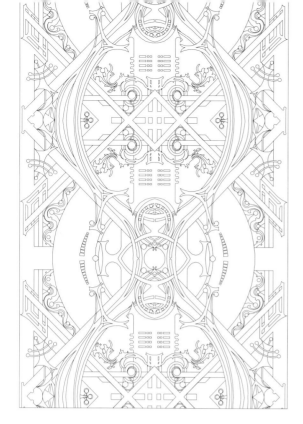

Building Mural Ghetto

canals tunnels (plumbing the body of the land)   clogged
pier
storms fires (FOLLY!)   *folies*
pseudea / alethea

Kinney made his fortune with Sweet Caporal cigarettes.

smoke (HAUNTING)

Educated in Europe, fluent in several languages including Latin, wrote books including *The Conquest of Death*, *Forest and Water*, and *Money*.

Founded Venice-of-America—as traders came to West Africa—to make money and art out of "native lack."

"His lofty dream envisioned a town built around a network of canals, with rich Italian-flavored architecture—a town dedicated to learning and artistic and cultural experience. At first he called it St. Mark's, but he changed the name to Venice-of-America."

Moran and Sewell, *Fantasy*, 11–12.

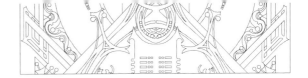

6. *Canal in the 1900s*

7. *Canal in the 1980s*

1904

canals and tunnels

Fanning out from a lagoon, a Grand Canal (half a mile long, 70 feet wide, 4 feet deep) and a fan shaped network of others (40 feet wide, 4 feet deep) with Venetian-style bridges over them, tied into the ocean through two large pipes under Windward Avenue so that the tides would freshen the system twice a day. Interconnecting tunnels under the alleyways to hide power lines and pump hot salt water to the hotelrooms.

pier with auditorium and hotels

St. Mark's, loosely modeled on the Doge's Palace. The Ship Hotel, replica of the galleon of Juan Cabrillo who landed near Malibu in 1542.

1905

Renaissance culture

Kinney announces the Summer Assembly, representing "the best in modern thought and art."

storm

Wrecked the pier and damaged the auditorium. Project called "Kinney's **Folly**."

Pier repaired in time for Grand Opening, July 4.

High culture doesn't sell. Low culture does.

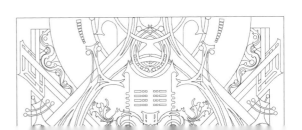

8. Post Office mural detail.
Amusements including Dragon Bamboo Slide.

1900s thru 1920s

folie house of pleasure, madness'

Midway Plaisance around lagoon offers *läppish* substitutes for foreign places and pleasures. *Smallest and Most Perfect Woman in the World. Streets of Cairo* with camel ride through reproduction of Algazera Plaza in Cairo. *Last Days of Pompeii. Dragon Bamboo Slide.*

"Tent City" **(woven walls)** near Plaisance is huge success.

canals

Canals provide insufficient flushing of the sewage.

Chronic clogging.

1925

death

Kinney dies in November. His power grip on Venice had earned him the title of "**Doge**."

fire

One month later, pier catches fire.

1929

canals

Canals filled up in the summer, right before the "Crash." Those south of Venice Blvd. left flowing. Return of "unstable sands and marshlands."

1930s and 1940s

ghetto

> Deterioration. Racial layers: elderly Jews in retirement homes, Blacks, Chicanos.
>
> Clashes between servicemen and "zoot suiters" in 1943.
>
> Return of "lack" in the body of land.

1950s

Beats

> "Lawrence Lipton chronicled the coffee houses, personal searches, artists and ennui of 'Venice West' in his book *The Holy Barbarians.*"   —Moran and Sewell, *Fantasy,* 94.
>
> Return of outsiders to make money and art from "native lack."

1960s

Hippies

1970s and 1980s

drugs, gangs, Oakwood ghetto

buildings, murals

9. 72 Market St., Morphosis. Pulley detail.

"That's when I moved to Venice. I'd never lived there, but I knew plenty of people who did, and the community suited my tastes. The air was clean. I was stimulated by the many interesting people, the variety of people. And Venice was close to my sailboat. But once I moved in, I discovered that some of my Hollywood and Beverly Hills friends wouldn't visit me here. Too dangerous, they said, and they may have been right."

—Tony Bill
Movie producer
Co-owner 72 Market St. restaurant

10. A "palazzo" on the Howland canal, remembering Venice screening the ghetto.

11. Does the arched window of "hacienda" see the Chicano ghetto?

148

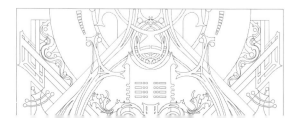

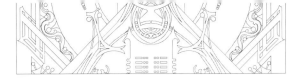

St. Mark's Hotel and Mural

12. St. Mark's Hotel in the 1900s.

13. St. Mark's Hotel and Mural in the 1970s.

In an uncanny, chronologically double movement, the St. Mark's recalls its past in its present condition. It traces a line back to its own origin in its deterioration from it.

Yet authorship haunts the building as a "revisitation of a power thought dead"—the authority to preserve the power of origination against the tide of temporal decay. So says the mural that has been applied to the side the the hotel.

14. View east mirrored in St. Mark's mural.

Insisting on the power of the St. Mark's to house a given moment, even as time passes away, the east elevation mural reflects its view of Hal's Pharmacy, the Four-Square Church, and the mountains beyond. In supplementing the mnemonic capacity of its building, the sub-architectural mural would exceed it.

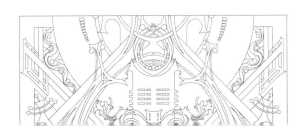

Ann Bergren

Queen Anne Mansion

15. *Queen Anne Mansion.*

At the heart of the Oakwood ghetto on Broadway, this still lovely Victorian mansion admits—in the deterioration of its exterior and the beaten-up easy-chairs on its front porch—its fall from social superiority to who-knows-what current depths. Who knows?

The interior knows—so the four mail boxes beside the door intimate. It is a house doubly haunted by traces of past grandeur and by the lack that its foreign style was built to cover.

Wesley House Mural

16. Wesley House Mural.

Before the horror inside reveals itself, the sub-architectural art of the mural comes to ward off the walls' unveiling.

Opposite the Baptist Church on Broadway, the mural of the Oakwood House builds a temple to community-building through sports. The stylized and exaggerated shape of its basketball player bespeak the energy and aesthetic confidence of rap music. Like an athletic belt hiding the *sexe* of its owner, the Classicizing arches—displaced from St. Mark's—screen not only the crack dealers and gangs in the area, but the steroids the local athletes may be taking.

151

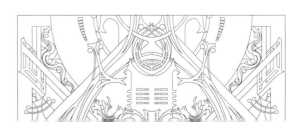

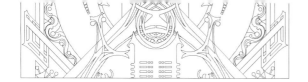

17. Dixon Studio, Westminster elevation.

18. Dixon Studio, 6th St. elevation.

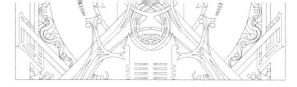

Dixon Studio, Brian Alfred Murphy

Waging an uneasy peace with its neighborhood, the walls of the nearby Dixon Studio stand as architectural prophalactics. Who can tell what is inside?

Muse-like they defy discovery of their desire, with a mnemonic face of socially undecidable layers: a haunting remnant of when the apartments within were the "Ritz" and a storefront over-written with the marks of its "adjancy." The ambiguity is symptomatic of what it screens.

Behind the facade is the home and studio of a high-style photographer, turning its other face (its other *"Decke"*) onto a scene of wind swept fir trees that might be Santa Cruz.

19. Dixon Studio, Deck.

Screening the ghetto by aestheticization, its graphic "trifles" sold as hip, inner-city fortress fashion—until recently, when the graffiti had to be painted over so that the owner could get insurance).

Again, *pseudea homoia etumoisin* (re)turns the *alethea* of its contiguity. But not before the architect/developer of the property—another in the long line of Kinney's successors—made art and money out of the ghetto's lack.

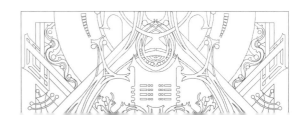

Indiana St. Apartments, Frank Gehry

20. Indiana St. Apartments.

"I'm more Classical than people realize," Gehry has said.

In his Indiana St. apartments, the architect monumentalizes the materials and forms, "the last impression before the uncanny and traumatic one."

Addition, Brian Alfred Murphy

21. *Indiana St. Apartments Addition.*

      As the St. Mark's mural saves itself by supplementing the mnemonic authority of the hotel, the Indiana St. Apartments addition forestalls oblivion through exposed ligature with another Venetian Classic.

      The transparent passage between host and parasite constructs a reciprocal memory-flow, recapitulating the working of Kinney's mind on the Post Office mural in recalling Venice, Italy's "Bridge of Sighs."

155

22. *Bridge of Sighs.*

1920s Remodel, Brian Alfred Murphy

22. 1920s Craftsman-style remodel with addition.

Another exercise in exposed architectural memory, the addition to this remodel accords to built *pseudea* its always partial truth. Leaving its origin unassimilated, the supplementary structure returns the Muses' transcendent knowledge as an always "detotalized totality."

There was always more before.

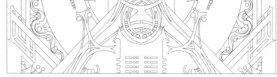

Bibliography

BASTEN, F. *Santa Monica Bay: The First 100 Years.* Los Angeles: Douglas-West, 1974.

EDINGER, CLAUDIO. *Venice Beach.* Photographs by Claudio Edinger. Introduction by Charles Lockwood. New York: Abbeville, 1985.

FREUD, SIGMUND. "Femininity." *New Introductory Letters on Psycho-analysis. Standard Edition* Vol. 22. (1933): 112–135.

_____. "Fetishismus." *SE* Vol. 21. (1927): 152–157.

_____. "The Sexual Abberations: Unsuitable Substitutes for the Sexual Object-Fetishism." *Three Essays on the Theory of Sexuality. SE* Vol. 7. (1905): 153–155.

_____. "Childhood Memories and Screen Memories." *Psychopathology of Everyday Life. SE* Vol. 6. (1901): 43–52.

_____. "Screen Memories." *SE* Vol. 3. (1899): 303–322.

NIETZSCHE, FRIEDRICH. "Preface to the Second Edition." of *The Gay Science* in *Friedrich Nietzsche, Samtliche Werke.,* Vol. 3. Edited by G. Colli and M. Montinari. Berlin and New York: Walter de Gruyter (1967–1977): 345–352.

MORAN, T. and T. SEWELL. *Fantasy by the Sea: A Visual History of the American Venice..* Culver City, CA: Peace Press, 1979.

PIETZ, WILLIAM. "The Problem of the Fetish, I." *Res 9* (Spring1985): 5–17 and "The Problem of the Fetish, II" *Res 13* (Spring 1987): 23–45.

SCHMIDT-BRUMMER, HORST. *Venice, California: An Urban Fantasy.* New York: Grossman, 1973.

SEMPER, GOTTFRIED. "Structural Elements of Assyrian-Chaldean Architecture," in Chapter 10 of "Comparative Building Theory." *Gottfried Semper: In Search of Architecture.* Translated by W. Herrman. Cambridge, MA: MIT Press, 1984

STANTON, JEFFREY. "*Coney Island of the Pacific,*" *Venice of America.* Los Angeles: Donahue, 1987.

_____. *Venice of America. 1905–1930.* Venice, CA: Ars Publications, 1980.

VIDLER, ANTHONY. "The Architecture of the Uncanny: The Unhomely Houses of the Romantic Sublime." *Assemblage* 5 (Cambridge, MA: MIT Press, 1987): 7–29.

William, Sweet. *Venice of America: The American Dream, Come True.* Venice, Ca.: Constitutional Capers, 1973.

Illustrations

1. Jeffrey Stanton, *Venice of America. 1905-1930,* 2.
2. Stanton, *Venice of America,* 19.
3. Christine M. Havelock *Hellenistic Art,* Greenwich, CT: New York Graphic Society Ltd. (n.d.): fig. 130.
4. Photograph by author.
5. Ibid.
6. Stanton, *Venice of America,* 40.
7. Photograph by author.
8. Ibid.
9. Ibid.
10. Ibid.
11. Ibid.
12. Stanton, *Venice of America,* 18.
13. Postcard, Venice, CA.
14. Photograph by author.
15. Ibid.
16. Ibid.
17. Ibid.
18. Ibid.
19. Ibid.
20. Ibid.
21. Ibid.
22. John Ruskin, *The Stones of Venice* (Boston: Little, Brown & Co., 1981) 173.

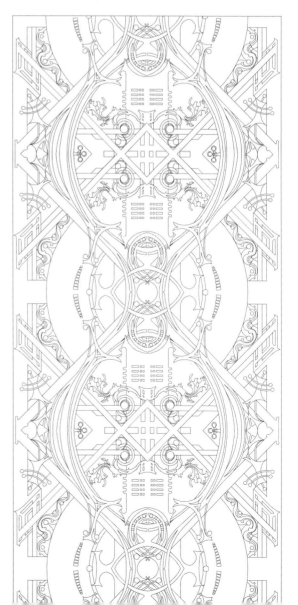

JEFFREY KIPNIS

Freudian Slippers

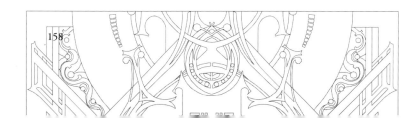

I was initially very reluctant to participate in the fetish conference. First of all, I had given very little thought to the subject aside from what I had read. Second, it seemed to me that there was something fishy about the fetish, something fishy about architecture borrowing yet another concept for commodification from the so-called strong disciplines of psychoanalysis, literary criticism and philosophy. Finally, it seemed to me that if anyone in architecture could do justice to the theme, it would be not me but Mark Wigley or Jennifer Bloomer, both of whom approach the subject in their work.

I said as much to the conference organizers, who responded that all that was required was an informal talk. They were indeed also considering Bloomer but had decided to ask me first. As I often do in such circumstances, I called friends to see what they thought. Typically, I call either Peter Eisenman or Mark Wigley, but in this case I opted not to contact either of them for the time being. Presumably, if I agreed to participate, I would likely refer to the work of one or the other during my talk. Instead I called Michael Hays who immediately agreed that it made much more sense for Bloomer to speak. Catherine Ingraham also affirmed that Bloomer was a much better choice. Finally I called Bloomer. When told of the invitation, she asked, *"Why did they invite you? They should have invited me!"* Now resolute in my decision, I called the fetish people back, but before I could decline I had a sudden insight into the possibilities for architecture in relation to the fetish. Perhaps I did indeed have some thoughts that might be of interest.

Before I share my thoughts on the fetish, consider these models submitted in the recent invitational competition for a convention center for Columbus, Ohio. After some fifteen design teams were screened, four were chosen to participate, led by Peter Eisenman, Michael Graves, Wesley Jones, and Barton Myers. The architects were specifically charged with designing a *"unique convention center"*—the contradiction in terms notwithstanding—to be built in time for the city's 1992 celebration of the 500th anniversary of Christopher Columbus's exploration of North America.

The oxymoron—a unique convention center—invites us to consider the competition under the aegis of the fetish, for the logic of fetishization describes the becoming unique of the conventional, the movement from cheap to priceless, from arbitrary to necessary, from commonplace to idol. Furthermore, this is no mere play on words; anyone familiar with the competition can verify to what extreme convention center experts insist that convention centers be conventional.

1.

Anyone who knows Wigley or Eisenman will understand my reaction when "shiftiest" showed up as the only anagram of "fetishist." It was like an epiphany. I knew I was onto something. However, the conference was on the fetish, not the fetishist, so, in my quest for greater rigor, I plugged in fetish, only to find that the word has no anagram. I was disappointed at first. Then two things occurred to me. First, this straightforward return to "fetish" from "fetish" was the very image of the philosophical desire for embodied meaning, which is also the desire for each thing to be what it properly is as such and lend itself to becoming nothing else. Second, I realized that my exercise was not successfully modeling the internal structure of excess. The essence of my argument is that the structure of excess internal to every object—whether word, thing, or idea—is both the possibility (and inevitability) of fetishization and the possibility of architectural design and that that same structure permanently threatens discourse, guaranteeing that while it proliferates meanings it never achieves full and

```
A:\>anagram fetish
ANAGRAM - version 2.2:PN
Copyright (c) Software Heaven, Inc. 1984
Portions Copyright (c) Wayne Holder 1981, 1982.
All rights reserved
NO WORDS MATCH PATTERN.
```

One of my reservations about the conference on fetish stemmed from my concern with architectural discourse's perverse habit of casually appropriating stylish concepts from strong discourses and subjecting them to slight if colorful repackaging. Consider, for example, the difference between the term "trace" in deconstruction, which marks a virtually unthinkable condition anterior to the production of anteriority, and the recent spate of appearances of the term in architectural discourse and design, where it operates quite superficially, often meaning nothing more than "footprint." Such cases are numerous, whether the originating discourse is structuralism, neo-Marxism, or another.

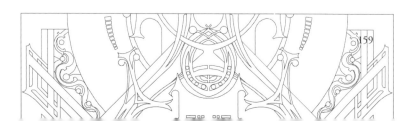

2.

A:\>anagram fetish?
ANAGRAM - version 2.2:PN
Copyright (c) Software Heaven, Inc. 1984
Portions Copyright (c) Wayne Holder 1981, 1982.

FISHNET   SHIFTED   SHIFTER

univocal meaning. A certain pattern is worth noting here. Whenever a strong discourse such as philosophy encounters a property of an object that threatens its desire for objects to be what it wants them to be, it exteriorizes that property into the realm of psychology. For example, the pathology of sexual fetishization is, from philosophy's point of view, not a problem of philosophy but of psychopathology. Indeed, one must consider the psychological issues but also ask how an object such as a shoe lends itself to and participates in such psychologies. This question, which philosophy must beg for its own survival, is nonetheless philosophical. In any case, I needed something in the exercise to model this issue of intrinsic excess. Fortunately, as I looked further into the anagramming program, I found that it allowed for "wildcard" letters. By adding a question mark to the entry, the program would look for anagrams of the word plus the wild card letter.

While many have complained about this flaw of architectural discourse, no one to my knowledge has done more forceful work on this strong/weak relationship than Mark Wigley who, through reading strategies made available by deconstruction and post-structuralism, proposes a kind of arche-contract between strong discourse and architectural discourse. In this contract strong discourse structures itself around and gains its very strength from a metaphysical appeal to an entire genus of architectural metaphors—most importantly, the inside/outside dichotomy—while architectural discourse remains weak and superficially derivative. In return, the architectural object stays under the purview of

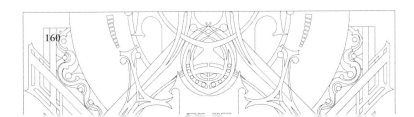

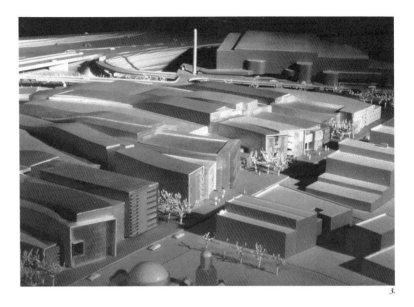

3.

The result was exactly the proliferation of meanings to be expected from thought on the generalized fetish. It came as no surprise that "fishiest" appeared early. Also worthy of note is the early emergence of autobiographical themes ("heftiest").

```
A:\>anagram fetish??
ANAGRAM - version 2.2:PN
Copyright (c) Software Heaven, Inc. 1984
Portions Copyright (c) Wayne Holder 1981, 1982.
All rights reserved
FETISHES          FIGHTERS          FISHIEST
FREIGHTS          HEFTIEST          HUFFIEST
SHIFTERS          SHIFTIER          SHRIFTED

A:\>anagram fetish???
ANAGRAM - version 2.2:PN
Copyright (c) Software Heaven, Inc. 1984
Portions Copyright (c) Wayne Holder 1981, 1982.
All rights reserved
FAITHLESS         FETISHISM         FETISHIST
FIFTIETHS         FILTHIEST         FLASHIEST
FLESHIEST         FORESIGHT         FORTIETHS
FRIGHTENS         FROTHIEST         GEARSHIFT
HEADFIRST         HEFTINESS         MAKESHIFT
SHIFTIEST         SHIFTLESS         WHITEFISH
```

architectural discourse and thus is rendered immune from scrutiny and theorization that could cast doubt on and destabilize the bona fides of the metaphysics of the architectural metaphor.

While I am persuaded and influenced by Wigley's argument, I have certain misgivings about it. For example, how is it that, from the outside, architectural discourse's weakness in relation to strong discourse seems easily demonstrable, while that same discourse operates from a position of strength and efficacy *within* architecture? In other words, how does architecture maintain its own self-image in the face of its obvious priorities and powers? On the other hand, rather than strong versus weak, primitive

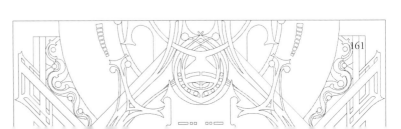

versus sophisticated, or perverse versus normal, could not the question actually be: How does a point of view that identifies weakness, primitivism, or perversity have confidence in its own strength, sophistication, and normative status?

The question of the relationship between discourse and design in architecture also remains problematic. Although Wigley would no doubt deny this, the presumption implicit in his thesis is that a more rigorous and subtle architectural discourse would in some way be measurably embodied in the object. Perhaps it is not so relevant, but I cannot get the example of Seurat out of my mind. Seurat derived his painting technique from his readings of a particular theory of vision. Today we know not only that Seurat interpreted the theory incorrectly, but that the theory itself was wrong! What does that say about the paintings, and, more interestingly, what does that say about what appears as discourse and what appears as practice in general? Perhaps consideration of the fetish will help to unfold these problems.

In the hands of August Compte, Karl Marx, Sigmund Freud, and even Friedrich Nietzsche (all authors of strong discourses) the fetish is a category of the object or object relationship that is in itself weak, primitive, or perverse. This status of the fetish obtains from viewing the fetish object or

A:\>anagram fetish????

ANAGRAM - version 2.2:PN

Copyright (c) Software Heaven, Inc. 1984

Portions Copyright (c) Wayne Holder 1981, 1982.

As I increased the play of excess, meanings—expected, unexpected, proper and improper—proliferated.

CHIEFTAINS	FARSIGHTED	FETISHISMS
FETISHISTS	FIFTEENTHS	FILTHINESS
FISHTAILED	FLESHLIEST	FLIGHTIEST
FLIGHTLESS	FREIGHTERS	FROTHIEST
GEARSHIFTS	INFIGHTERS	SHIFTINESS
SHOPLIFTED	SHOPLIFTER	SMITHFIELD
SOUTHFIELD	STARFISHES	THRIFTIEST
THRIFTLESS		

relationship as evidencing a displacement, a deviant shift from self-evident actuality. Thus, only from a self-confidence in the falseness of animistic beliefs can Compte call all primitive religions fetishisms; only from the point of view of knowing the actual value of labor exchange can Marx identify those distorted values and objectifications that he terms fetishisms of the commodity. And finally, only from the point of view of knowing a normal and proper object choice can Freud identify a sexual fetish. In each of these cases and in fact in every case in which the identification of a fetish is the identification of a status, which is to say in every case of a fetish, an object relationship is identified as a naive or pathological deviation from a presumed authentic referent. A real shoe is a thing properly exemplifying

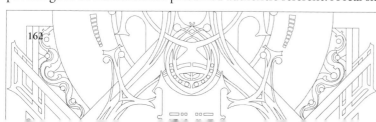

shoeness. It is a perversity for it to slip into any other meaning or for any other meaning, such as the mother's phallus, to slip into it.

This explains why the fetish is a juridical concept central to strong discourse, which depends for its strength on a steadfast and straightforward logic of authentic and verifiable reference. Even if that discourse would like to recover the fetish for its own use, it must know and be able to distinguish it. Recall for a moment the scene in Paul Valéry's *Eupalinos* in which Socrates chooses between architecture and philosophy as his life vocation. Socrates finds an unidentifiable object on the beach: for every possible identification, he finds confirming evidence in the object. Driven by anxiety caused not by insufficient evidence or lack of knowledge but rather by excess evidence and excess knowledge—which is to say, no knowledge at all as knowledge would like to know itself—Socrates abandons a relationship to the material world and takes up philosophy, where knowledge is knowledge, where one knows each thing as it is in itself ideally and exclusively. It might be said that what Valéry's Socrates confronts in his beachside epiphany is the irreducible excess of references engendered by all material objects, including not only things but spoken or written words. In other words, Socrates faces a fetish and is made anxious by his realization that this case is not a perversity but a general structure of all objects. In that case we identify

What single strand of thought could connect "afterbirths" to "bullfighters" but that of the fetish? Several issues must be stressed: this is not an exercise of words but rather—like architectural design—an exercise of the materiality of objects in relation to their ability to engender meanings.

A:\>anagram fetish?????
ANAGRAM - version 2.2:PN
Copyright (c) Software Heaven, Inc. 1984
Portions Copyright (c) Wayne Holder 1981, 1982.
All rights reserved

AFTERBIRTHS	FETISHISTIC	FLIGHTEINESS
FORESIGHTED	GUNFIGHTERS	HEFTINESSES
PATHFINDERS	PINFEATHERS	SHIFTLESSLY
SHOPLIFTERS	SPACEFLIGHT	SPENDTHRIFT
THRIFTINESS	TIGHTFISTED	

A:\>anagram fetish??????
ANAGRAM - version 2.2:PN
Copyright (c) Software Heaven, Inc. 1984
Portions Copyright (c) Wayne Holder 1981, 1982.
All rights reserved

BULLFIGHTERS	CHESTERFIELD	FAITHFULNESS
FARSIGHTEDLY	FATHERLINESS	FEATHERINESS
FILTHINESS	FLIGHTLESSLY	FREETHINKERS
FROTHINESSES	MIRTHFULNESS	RIGHTFULNESS
SHIFTINESSES	SPACEFLIGHTS	SPENDTHRIFTS
THRIFTLESSLY	WETHERSFIELD	WHIFFLETREES

a generalized fetish that escapes the notion of the juridical fetish, a bad substitute for the thing itself.

By now, everyone is familiar with how much deconstructionists love to wallow in perversity and deviation. Thus it comes as no surprise to find Derrida and others, particularly Ulmer, elevating the fetish from its lowly status as deviant exemplifier to the model par excellence for the general structure of referring necessarily anterior to and thus free from proper reference. In this case proper reference or authentic exemplification is thus only one of an excess of references always engendered by any referent. I should be somewhat careful here, for deconstruction does not call for a revolutionary reversal of value between proper reference and fetishistic or deviant reference; rather, it seeks to demonstrate that the structure that

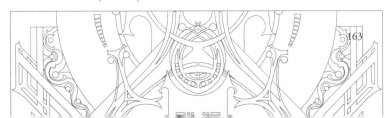

makes proper reference possible is already the structure of the possibility of fetish. Thus deconstruction is able to raise questions in general about the conditions of any object choice—for instance, the choice of an example in an argument and of the exemplariness of that choice acting as a precedent or source of propriety identifying as fetish mechanisms the analogies, homomorphisms, distortions, and abstractions necessary for any object to become properly exemplary. The goal of such a demonstration is neither reproduction nor transformative production (i.e., a law that neither radically prohibits fetishes nor radically valorizes fetishes). Rather, what is called for is a respect and even an indulgence in fetish mechanisms as fetish mechanisms, as weak, as precise, to see what they engender—on the principle that what appropriately stands as a normal, powerful, and sophisticated mechanism cannot escape analysis as a fetishization.

In so doing, deconstruction mounts a powerful critique of a metaphysics of embodiment, that any object embodies a meaning. It does this, however, without producing a "pure formalism," sidestepping the ancient form/meaning dialectic. Rather, deconstruction delimits what might be called an engendering formalism in that form is always already excessive, an open-ended engendering, the dream of strong discourse.

A:\>anagram fetish???????

ANAGRAM - version 2.2:PN

Copyright (c) Software Heaven, Inc. 1984

Portions Copyright (c) Wayne Holder 1981, 1982.

CHESTERFIELDS	FAITHLESSNESS	FLIGHTINESS
FOUNTAINHEADS	FRANCHISEMENT	FRIGHTFULNESS
PRIZEFIGHTERS	REFURBISHMENT	SHIFTLESSNESS
UNTHRIFTINESS		

A:\>anagram fetish????????

ANAGRAM - version 2.2:PN

Copyright (c) Software Heaven, Inc. 1984

Portions Copyright (c) Wayne Holder 1981, 1982

DELIGHTFULNESS	FAITHFULNESSES	FARSIGHTEDNESS
FATHERLINESSES	FEATHERWEIGHTS	FLIGHTLESSNESS
FORESHORTENING	FORTHRIGHTNESS	FRANCHISEMENTS
INSIGHTFULNESS	MIRTHFULNESSES	REFURBISHMENTS
RIGHTFULNESSES	THRIFTLESSNESS	UNFAITHFULNESS

Second, the exercise never leaves the realm of meaning—each word engenders meaning—though no connection of proper meanings exists among the words. No nonsense words are produced, which would have been analogous to the avant-garde's ambition to produce new meaning via a *tabula rasa*. The connection is neither meaningful nor meaningless. It results from the internal excess of the object opening that object to the decision-making force of a provisional decision frame. Are the connections between the word *fetish*, the context of this conference in an architecture school, and the appearance of the word *fountainheads*, meaningful? If this is mere coincidence, then must we not look to the structure of the participants in that coincidence, or, said differently, is not the structure of the fetish also the structure that not only enables but guarantees coincidence?

Returning to Wigley's argument, we can now identify a conspicuous omission. In theorizing about the absence in rigor and subtlety in architectural discourse and thus identifying architectural discourse as a field of fetishization run amok, Wigley fails to note the proscription on and paradoxical dependence on the use of fetish mechanisms from strong discourse. He fetishizes the strength of strong discourse. His argument should at the same time call for weak, primitive, and deviant practices—architectural activities—in strong discourses. Recalling that the term *fetish* comes from the Portuguese *feticio*, literally "something made," this amounts to doing with strong discourse what architecture and

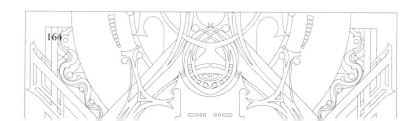

architectural discourse already does: manipulating and remanipulating in not necessarily proper or rigorous fashion innate or borrowed materials.

When I first started working on this talk, I knew that I wanted to do something other than simply put forward the beginnings of a considered argument about the relationship between architecture and the generalized fetish. Considering the panel members, I thought that my only hope of making a contribution was to find an example or model of the operation of the generalized fetish. I knew that for the example to work, it would have to seem a little ridiculous, a little perverse, a little weak, a little irrelevant, and finally a little solipsistic. On the other hand, to make the point the example would also have to engender insights into either my arguments, the convention center competition, or both. These accidental insights would, like a fetish, have the character of being real but not properly real. Desperate, I remembered that my computer has a neat little program for anagramming words that generates every possible anagram corresponding to each entry in its 200,000 word list. So with nothing more than Eisenman and Wigley on my mind, I plugged in the word *fetishist* to see what would happen.

Because the exercise in general and the wildcard feature in particular are but models of the structure of the fetish (by its very nature, such a structure could never be revealed) the proliferation inevitably comes to an end. (In life, of course, the proliferation is interminable and uncontrollable.)

A:\>anagram fetish????????
ANAGRAM - version 2.2:PN
Copyright (c) Software Heaven, Inc. 1984
Portions Copyright (c) Wayne Holder 1981, 1982.

ENFRANCHISEMENT	FORESIGHTEDNESS	FRIGHTFULNESSES
STANDOFFISHNESS		

A:\>anagram fetish?????????
ANAGRAM - version 2.2:PN
Copyright (c) Software Heaven, Inc. 1984
Portions Copyright (c) Wayne Holder 1981, 1982.

DELIGHTFULNESSES	DISFRANCHISEMENT	ENFRANCHISEMENTS
FAINTHEARTEDNESS	FARSIGHTEDNESSES	FASHIONABILITIES

What is at stake in this issue of the generalized fetish for architecture? In the broadest perspective, a great deal. It raises serious questions, for example, about an intellectual tradition that would ground architectural argument—whether history, theory, or criticism—in the capacity of an object to arbitrate as example. Insofar as every argument subtends and restricts the excess inherent in objects in order to achieve its capacity to exemplify, it fetishizes the object.

Thus, also at stake is the entire tradition of design that strives to uphold and realize the ambitions of that intellectual tradition. The generalized fetish raises questions about the systems of precedent—typological, morphological, or otherwise—forming the proprietary structures of

pattern-book design methodologies, as well as the decisive factors—function, context, etc.—performing the equivalent role in analysis/synthesis design methodologies. At the very least, these methodologies would be obliterated to shift their discourse of legitimation from the epistemological to the overtly political.

These complex and important issues require a careful, rigorous, and dedicated unfolding beyond the scope of this paper. To close, then, I raise a far more limited consequence and speak to a design agenda implied in this discussion.

A:\>anagram fetish???????????

ANAGRAM - version 2.2:PN

Copyright (c) Software Heaven, Inc. 1984

Portions Copyright (c) Wayne Holder 1981, 1982.

All rights reserved

DEHUMIDIFICATIONS   DISFRANCHISEMENTS   FORESIGHTEDNESSES
GRANDFATHERLINESS

A:\>anagram fetish???????????

ANAGRAM - version 2.2:PN

Copyright (c) Software Heaven, Inc. 1984

Portions Copyright (c) Wayne Holder 1981, 1982.

All rights reserved

NO WORDS MATCH PATTERN.

A:\>anagram fetish????????????

ANAGRAM - version 2.2:PN

Copyright (c) Software Heaven, INc. 1984

Portions Copyright (c) Wayne Holder 1981, 1982.

All rights reserved

STRAIGHTFORWARDNESS

The exercise finally came to a close, the computer reported "No words match pattern." I decided, however, to press on, for, although the exercise had accomplished all that I hoped for, I could not shake the sense that there should have been more. I added a thirteenth question mark. A fitting conclusion: not only would the Nietzchean recognize in this the eternal return—remember the straightforward response with which we began—every deconstructionist would delight in the discovery of the fetish within straightforwardness.

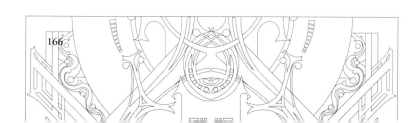

The structure of the object as generalized fetish guarantees that once meaning is set in motion at all—and every disposition of material form sets meaning into motion—the proliferation of other meanings, whether desirable or not, can neither be predetermined nor arrested. What is at stake here for architecture? In the broadest perspective, a great deal. As I have already discussed, problems arise, for example, for an intellectual tradition that would ground architectural argument—whether history, theory or criticism—on the capacity of an object to arbitrate debate as *prima facie* evidence. Insofar as every argument subtends the excess of reference inherent in the structure of an object in order to call upon its capacity to exemplify, that argument fetishizes the object as some "thing."

Thus, also at stake are theories of design which strive to realize the ambitions of the intellectual tradition. The generalized fetish raises questions about the agendas that underwrite the theory of precedents which form the basis for pattern-book methods and the theory of parameters which performs the equivalent role in analysis/synthesis methods. At the very least, each of these methodologies would need to rewrite its discourse of legitimation in terms more political than ontological. The significance of this shift cannot be underestimated; as an intrinsically negotiated practice, architecture is constructed—fundamentally and inextricably—as a discourse of legitimation.

Two issues are perhaps more immediately interesting for contemporary design, however. First, implied within the thought of the generalized fetish is the emergence of a third design methodology. Methodologies, of course, are only theories of methods; it goes without saying that no design practice is entirely faithful to one methodology. It is a matter of emphasis, for there is always an analysis/synthesis component to every pattern-book approach, and vice versa. In a sense, Colin Rowe's demonstrations of this interplay in *The Mathematics of the Ideal Villa* marked the moment when design theory and design ideology cleaved. As the ideological debate which fueled the initial antagonism between pattern-book and analysis/synthesis theories grew increasingly unpersuasive and unable to command methodological allegiance, the compound practices which we collectively term "post-modernism" began to borrow freely from both methodologies.

In its articulation of the object as an exorbitance of reference in essence, the mediation on the generalized fetish suggests that *grafting*[A] can be elaborated as an independent design methodology. As with pattern-book and analysis/synthesis, *grafting* names a large and diverse catalogue of methods and practices. Basically, however, *grafting* consists of attaching a prepared but not necessarily well-motivated object to the site and elaborating on the resulting connections, liaisons and affiliations which the graft inevitably engenders as an effect of the structural excess of reference.

As is to be expected, *grafting* will have been already implicit in both pattern-book and analysis/synthesis methodologies. It becomes explicit and independent as a design methodology when the question of the premeditated motives underwriting the initial graft is thematized. The ability of either a typological precedent or a bubble diagram to yield an appropriate design already depends on the logic of the graft, i.e., the capacity of the initial object to engage a context in terms beyond the authority of its initial selection. The questions raised by grafting as a methodology, on the other hand, are to what extent and to what desired effect might any arbitrary initial condition productively graft to a given site and program.

The second consequence for contemporary design of the generalized fetish structure might be understood as the formulation of a new aspiration for architectural meaning. Traditional models for the role of meaning in the design process circulate within a field delimited by *monosemy*, the embodiment of a single overriding meaning, and *polysemy*, the embodiment of many layers of different meanings.

Obviously, the governable slippage of meaning guaranteed by the structure of the generalized fetish implies that, in principle, the embodiment of meaning(s) as such cannot be achieved. Indeed, the

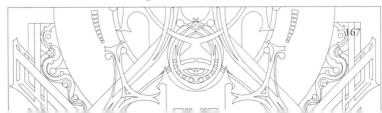

very concept of embodiment, whose constellation (*incarnation, concretization, materialization, incorporation,* etc., etc., etc.,) presides over the most diverse design theories with astonishing vigor, is undermined as metaphysical by a contemplation of the fetish. The reader need look no further than this very volume to discover just how pervasive the commitment of criticism is to the metaphysical belief that meaning is embodied in material-form and that it in turn can be extricated and revealed.[B]

On the other hand, the notion of an essential excess of reference raises the possibility of a design process seeking a material-form ensemble which makes no overt gesture towards embodiment, but which instead gives as much play as possible to the engenderment of meanings without either endorsement or the arbitration of contradiction. In deconstruction, Derrida has named the possibility *dissemination,* a term which plays on that word's ability to mean at once the production and distribution as well as the confoundment and interruption of meaning.

Again, every work is in principle disseminating. The effects of monosemy and polysemy are achieved for a period of time by mounting resistance to the inevitable slippage and degradation of intended meaning. Thus, the stage is set for a fertile debate in contemporary design among monosemy, polysemy, and dissemination. A particularly clear engagement of conflict occurred in the Columbus Convention Center Competition.[C]

In its Convention Center scheme as in its other work, HHPJ take up the precariousness of architectural meaning as a problem to be confronted with aggressive monosemy. Virtually every aspect of the HHPJ project is dedicated to achieving a source of decisive, monovalent meaning. Wherever possible, potential links to the site, to the extended context and to a broader encyclopedia of references, architectural or otherwise, are truncated or narrowed.

The site for the Columbus Convention Center occupies the threshold between the large scale buildings of the downtown area and the small store-front commercial buildings and residential areas that characterize High Street as it continues north. Rather than negotiate the scale disjunction of the immediate context, the HHPJ scheme exacerbates it with a massive structure. The surface and material vocabulary are relentlessly monotonous, further detaching the building from the context by narrowing the range of architectural references to naked tectonics. Indeed, to ameliorate the stark, alien character of the project and to restore a gesture of applied ornament, "Welcome to Columbus" is literally written in flowers on the Center's grounds. Such signage operates to preserve the aloofness of the building at the very moment it forges its tentative link.

While HHPJ's strategy is to resist dissemination with a hyperbolic monolith so assertive as to be unshakable, the scheme by Michael Graves is a text-book example of polysemy. Graves embraces polysemy as a way out of the symbolic destitution characteristic of doctrinaire modernism. In addition, however, one can understand polysemy as a strategy for resistance to dissemination as follows: unwanted meanings and meaning slippage occurs when a building which has been designed to be understood in one interpretive frame lends itself to be read in another. Therefore, by anticipating the more significant, reading frames and embodying meaning in the project for each of those, slippage effects can be preempted and deferred.

Whether or not one loves or loathes Graves's histrionics, one cannot deny that, as with much of his work, this project is a tour de force of polysemic technique. So abundant and interwoven is the texture of this project that its many threads cannot be unraveled adequately in the space remaining to this discussion. At the level of the site diagram, a formal "H" is sheared longitudinally, the static side acting as a transition barrier to the exhibition space and the sheared side accreting elements to produce a cloister. In elevation, the shear is notated in the material painting of a shifted pediment. In plan, the shear engages a corner rotunda, which acts as both a traditional turning icon on the street as well as a formal hinge

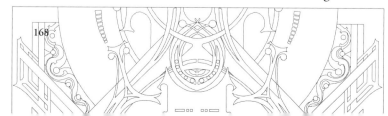

element transferring the dynamics of the shear into the pre-existing rotation of the Hyatt Hotel of the Ohio Center. The effect of this aspect of the project is to incorporate the major existing elements in the immediate context into a single, formalist diagram.

Graves's familiar ornamental catalogue and service devices are evident, including the material/color palette, the pastiche of historical allusions and honorific elements as well as references to pop and pattern and decoration painting. Also in full force is his inclination to a symbolic representation *à la architecture parlant* of a signature feature of the project. Here, this takes the form of various gestures to the fact that the Columbus Convention Center is scheduled to open in association with the City's celebration of the 500th anniversary of the voyages of Christopher Columbus. Thus, Columbus's Santa Maria stands in a fountain on a pedestal, his three-ship flotilla recurs as three canopied kiosks, the roof of the exhibition hall is configured as a sail with masts, and the cross-bar element to the "H" form is outfitted as a modern ocean liner, presumably completing an "ocean voyages then and now" motif.

It would be interesting in a more extensive treatment of the Graves's project in the context of a reflection on the fetish to consider how deeply this project depends on fetish mechanisms, both in the possibility of the elements to enter into polysemic relationships as well as in the formation of Graves's vocabulary. So implicated is the fetish structure in polysemic design that Eisenman's earliest efforts to respond to deconstruction—his so called archeological or scaling projects—failed to attend the difference between *polysemy* and *dissemination*. His projects of that period such as the Wexner Center pursued the embodiment of multiple meanings to an extreme.

In his recent *weak form* projects, however, Eisenman's work seems to be taking initial steps toward an architecture of dissemination, at least insofar as large-scale institutional works are able to be moved in this direction. In traditional terms, the Eisenman project possesses neither the strength of statement of the HHPJ scheme nor the contrapuntal complexity of Graves's. Though vaguely reminiscent of some Expressionist architectures, the scheme does not particularly enjoy any quotational force. At first reading the work seems motivated purely by aesthetic considerations, since the exotic, veriform tendrils which lace and mat into the massing of the project contribute neither a typological ground, a legible iconography nor a clarifying geometry to the existing conditions.

On the other hand, when interrogated for relationships which would suggest content beyond its aesthetic properties, the project yields a different, uneasy order of "confirmation." Morphologically, it is not clear whether the massing is additive (reading the laced tendrils from High Street east) or articulated monolith (reading the project from its homogeneous west edge toward High Street.) Moreover, the independent sectional space for the interior does not arbitrate between these two contradictory massing schemas as the residue of the body-geometry of one or the other.

Contextually, the project seems to extend the system of horizontal extrusion established by the bank of store-front buildings fronting the project across High Street, though this logic breaks down in the eventual gesture, knitting and unifying the extruded bars. On the other hand, the project also reads somewhat as a concretization of the adjacent highway system geometry, though this reading too is subverted as much as confirmed. Iconographically, the project recalls the footprint of the railroad track interchange that once occupied the site, though no other aspect of the project, e.g., ornament or material, supports the reading. In fact, the allusion is so indefinite as to be ephemeral at best.

Given the constraints imposed on the program, the project seems at once to confirm and deny various interpretive incursions. In this sense it cannot be said to embody multiple meanings; it is neither meaningful nor meaningless; it enters into affiliations with many reading frames while subverting each and confirming none. But does this not move towards the character one would expect of the generalized fetish, a disseminating architecture? Where monosemic architecture strives to achieve a "yes, no" and

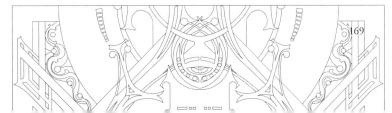

polysemic architecture strives to provide a "yes, yes" response to interpretive interrogation, the architecture of dissemination should always engender a "yes, but . . . ."

While always available to criticism of specifics, monosemic and polysemic architectures in general enjoy a well-formulated values debate and flourish under the auspices of a well-rehearsed discourse of legitimation. Insofar as it moves to undermine the terms and conditions which would make those dialogues possible, the architecture of dissemination, on the other hand, cannot simply give itself over to such familiar negotiations of desirability and deservedness. Therefore, beyond the fact of its possibility—again, a fact which is more political than ontological—what circumstance calls for and supports such an architecture? Deferring a thorough treatment of this question for the time being, let me suggest in passing that its answers will carry us to a raveling of that fetish of fetishes, the "city" and, though I have repeatedly invoked the term "political," to a dismantling of the constellation of the *polis* in favor of more textured, technological and provisional models of aggregation.

Another caution. Recall at the beginning of this essay, I was concerned to forestall the instrumentalization of the *fetish* as a new conceptual tool for strong discourse. In that regard, my thesis has been that the structure of the fetish, a structure of essential excess, is both the possibility of design and the impossibility of strong discourse to comprehend and govern design. The scene of the fetish therefore is precisely the arena where design is pitted against discourse. Yet, in my discussion of methodology as well as monosemy, polysemy, and dissemination, I have to some extent undermined my own position. To correct this, allow me to return one last time to design.

By virtue of the extremes of its three entries, the Columbus Convention Center Competition provides an interesting snapshot of a current design debate. But we should not make the error of assuming therefore that these competition entries form a metonymy for that debate, i.e., stand in as part sufficiently representing whole. Perhaps more than any other single device, the delusion of metonymy, which amounts to the violent reduction of excess, is the pre-eminent weapon of strong discourse.

Hence, we should be wary of an argument which configures three projects as examples of a comprehensive theoretical field delimited by three concepts. Were we to shuffle in certain other projects we would find that each caused the conceptual structure we have outlined to proliferate well beyond the boundaries of the inquiry, pushing the notion of dissemination to its limits and going from there in unexpected directions, much as the *fetish* anagrams do with each addition of a wildcard letter.

Though every architectural project has this capability not every one has this effect. Most do not. To the extent that a design operates to affirm the status of some strong discourse or another through embodiment or exemplification, it must limit its own abilities to engender this possibility.

Allow me to end, then, with an unadorned list of projects each of which I believe radically exceeds the current capacities of strong discourse, architectural or otherwise, to comprehend it. Because strong discourse prefers the security of projects it already understands, none has been treated in any depth; most have received no consideration at all. It would be wrong to say that each is therefore a theory waiting to be written; rather, it must be said that each are theories waiting to be engendered.

Hejduk: *The Berlin Masque*
Nouvel: *Tokyo Opera House project*
Eisenman: *University of Cincinnati DAAP edition*
Shirdel & Zago: *Los Angeles Civic Center District Masterplan*
Gehry: *Vitra Factory and Museum Complex* D
Libeskind *Berlin National Museum addition*
Koolhaas: *Bibliothèque Nationale project*

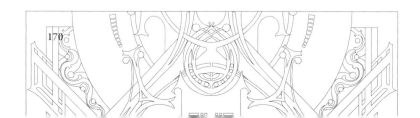

Though *grafting* is a procedure employed extensively in deconstruction, it is nowhere conceived in deconstruction as in methodological terms. Indeed, the very notion of a methodology is anathematic to deconstruction. Nevertheless, I have borrowed the term because a methodological treatment of *grafting* would resonate strongly with both the ad hoc practices engaged in by deconstruction as well as the argumentation in support of such procedures in that discourse. It goes without saying that a methodological treatment of *grafting* would therefore not read as a familiar and customary theory of the method.

A

Perhaps the most telling symptom of this delusion in academic writing is the obsession with the footnote. Freud's seminal analysis of foot fetishism as well as his speculations on multiple phallic images would no doubt prove invaluable resources in a treatment of this scholarly perversion.

B

An extended reading of this competition, elaborating in more depth upon the methodological and critical themes touched upon herein can be found in my essay, "Architectural Seme-Antics: Structure, Sign and Play in the Columbus Convention Center Competition," (*AD* publication pending).

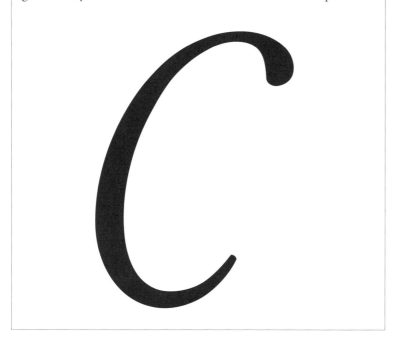

It is particularly interesting to note that, in the few essays which have considered this project at all, the entire focus is on the museum. None has considered the factory complex at all, though the most virulent aspects of the work are to be found in the relations engendered between the museum and the complex.

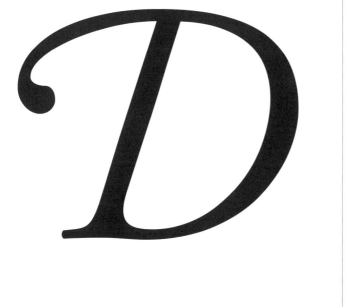

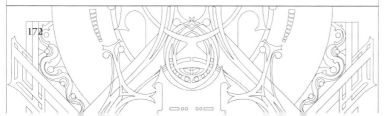

Illustrations

1.   Holt Hinshaw Pfau Jones. Columbus Convention Center Competition.
2.   Michael Graves. Columbus Convention Center Competition.
3.   Peter Eisenman. Columbus Convention Center Competition.

Author Biographies

EMILY APTER received her Ph.D. in Comparative Literature from Princeton University in 1983. She is currently an Associate Professor in the Department of French and Italian at the University of California, Davis. Her books include: *André Gide and the Codes of Homotextuality* (Stanford French and Italian Studies, Anma Libri, 1987), *Feminizing the Fetish: Psychoanalysis and Narrative Obsession in Turn-of-the-Century France* (Cornell University Press, Fall 1991) and *Fetishism as Cultural Discourse: Gender, Commodity and Vision*, co-edited with William Pietz (Forthcoming, Cornell University Press). Currently she is engaged in a book-length study: "Psychoanalysis and the French Colonial Archive: The Haremization Effect in North Africanist Discourse 1880–1931." She has published articles in *Assemblage, Ottagono, October, The National Women's Studies Association Journal, Critique, Poétique,* and *Romanic Review,* among others.

ANN BERGREN received her Ph.D. in Classical Philology from Harvard University in 1973 and is currently an Associate Professor of Classics at the University of California, Los Angeles and an Adjunct Instructor at the Southern California Institute of Architecture. She has published numerous articles and is currently finishing a book, *Architecture Gender Philosophy*.

JENNIFER BLOOMER teaches, writes about, practices, and worries about architecture. She received B.S., M.Arch., and Ph.D. degrees in architecture from the Georgia Institute of Technology. She is an Associate Professor at the University of Iowa and the Director of Graduate Studies, a former Fellow of the Chicago Institute for Architecture and Urbanism and author of numerous articles and a book, *Desiring Architecture: The Scrypt of Joyce and Piranesi*, forthcoming from the Yale University Press. Currently, she is completing an architectural project to be documented in a book called *Tabbles of Bower: Abodes of Theory and Flesh*.

TRACY E. BROWN is a Ph.D. student in English at Princeton University. Her interests are in contemporary American literature, women's novels, feminist theory, cultural studies, horror films and fiction. Her dissertation is on contemporary gothic fiction.

HAL FOSTER is a critic of art, architecture, and culture, and is currently an art history instructor at the Whitney Independent Study Program. He co-founded the journal *Zone* and has been senior editor of *Art in America*. Foster has edited several books including *The Anti-Aesthetic: Essays in Post Modern Culture* and two Dia Foundation books. His own book of collected essays is called *Recodings*.

JEFFREY KIPNIS is Assistant Professor of Theory and Design in the Department of Architecture, Ohio State University, Columbus and a member of the Los Angeles design firm Shirdel, Zago, Kipnis. His publications include *In the Manor of Nietzsche*, a collection of aphorisms.

ROBERT E. SOMOL is an Associate Professor of Theory and Design at the University of Illinois, Chicago. He is working toward his Ph.D. at the University of Chicago, and has published numerous articles.

MARK WIGLEY received his B.Arch in 1979 and his Ph.D. in 1980 from the University of Auckland, New Zealand. He is currently a teacher at Princeton University, was a former fellow of the Chicago Institute of Architecture, and was an associate curator of the exhibition "Deconstructivist Architecture" at the Museum of Modern Art in New York City.

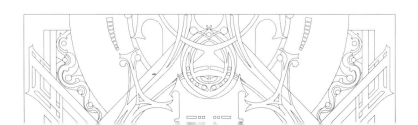

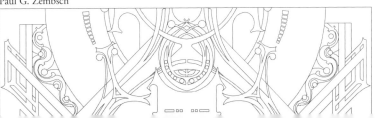